EARTH'S
last great places

EARTH'S
last great places

Noel Grove

Exploring The Nature Conservancy Worldwide

NATIONAL GEOGRAPHIC

WASHINGTON, D.C.

CONTENTS

*Thorns bristle on walking palm trees at
Pacaya-Samiria National Reserve in Peru.*

saving treasured lands

They are the Earth's natural treasures, lands and waters untarnished by human imprint— unpaved, unplowed, ungroomed.

THE NATURE CONSERVANCY CALLS THEM "LAST GREAT PLACES," and, for more than half a century, the Conservancy has been working to protect these precious lands and waters for us, for our children, and for their children.

The alternative is unthinkable. As Wallace Stegner reminds us, wilderness reassures us "of our sanity as creatures." Without it, we lose the settings and the scenery that help make us whole, the places that inspire us and remind us of life's simple pleasures. These are reasons enough to hold on to the last great places that remain.

My family and I support The Nature Conservancy because it recognizes both the value of nature and the needs of people. Working locally with communities, businesses, and individuals, the Conservancy makes people part of the answer to the complex conservation issues we face.

Long successful in setting aside special habitats, the Conservancy now takes the wider view of saving entire ecosystems, focusing on large functional landscapes that cross political borders and reach far beyond the boundaries of the Conservancy's preserves. Whether acting as an advisor to the governments of other countries or supporting local environmental organizations in our own backyard, the Conservancy is finding solutions that benefit both the land and the people who live there.

With each success, another piece of our natural heritage is preserved—a living scrapbook from which future generations will learn. The Nature Conservancy offers us the opportunity to create a legacy that will outlast us all. It's the most soulful kind of generosity we know.

Joanne Woodward

Kachemak Bay,
Alaska

Indian Boundary Prairies,
Illinois

Greater Yellowstone,
Wyoming

Upper Klamath Basin,
Oregon

Cosumnes River,
California

San Luis Valley,
Colorado

El Pinacaté &
Grand Desert de Altar,
Mexico

Lower San Pedro River,
Arizona

Sea of Cortés,
Mexico

Cuatro Ciénagas,
Mexico

Kamakou
Preserve,
Hawai'i

Waikamoi
Preserve,
Hawai'i

Palmyra Atoll

Sierra del Lacandon
National Park,
Guatemala

Galápagos Marine Reserve,
Ecuador

El Angel,
Ecuador

Konza
Prairie,
Kansas

Gila River,
New Mexico

NORTH
AMERICA

Upper Peninsula,
Michigan

Neversink River,
New York

Poconos,
Pennsylvania

Delaware Bay Shores,
New Jersey & Delaware

Jocassee Gorges,
North & South Carolina

ACE Basin,
South Carolina

Altamaha River,
Georgia

Florida Keys,
Florida

Rio Bravo Conservation
and Management Area,
Belize

Canaima National Park,
Venezuela

SOUTH
AMERICA

Guaraqueçaba,
Brazil

Arctic

Atlantic

Ocean

Pacific   Ocean

AN[T]

EARTH'S LAST GREAT PLACES

● a "Last Great Place" protected by
The Nature Conservancy and
featured in this book

miles
0   1000   2000   3000

0   1000   2000   3000
kilometers

Fragile habitats supporting unique wild plants
and animals still exist in hidden corners around the Earth.
Working with groups and individuals worldwide,
The Nature Conservancy seeks to protect these last great places
in the Americas, Asia, and the Pacific Islands.

THE PACIFIC

Nearly blotting out the sun, a manta ray glides near the surface in the Komodo Straits as two smaller fish tag along.

Healthy fire urchins in Horseshoe Bay on Rinca,
one of the Komodo Islands, gain the promise of a future
thanks to efforts to curtail destructive fishing practices.

rainbows
in the sea

∽

I never expected to see dragons except in fairy
tales. And I never expected to find a fairyland
underwater. Both exist in Indonesia's Komodo
archipelago 300 miles east of Bali. There, a string
of long extinct volcanoes protrudes from the ocean
like ridged scales on a dragon's back,
and on them prowl the world's largest lizards:
Komodo dragons that grow to nine-foot lengths
and dine on deer, wild pigs, water buffalo,
and even people if given the chance.

JUST A FEW YARDS AWAY FROM SANDS trodden by these remnants of the Cretaceous exists an underwater world of enchantment. Fed by upwellings from the Indian Ocean and by nutrient- and oxygen-rich currents swirling around the islands, the coral reefs of Komodo are among the richest in the world, the most colorful, and the most diverse. Some 260 species of coral extend their tentacles of red, yellow, blue, orange, rust, and forest green. Sponges of purples and golds, some 70 species, reach up like small cylindrical castles from the seafloor, and more than a thousand species of fish drift through the scene like a moving rainbow. Red fish, blue fish, green fish, yellow fish, multicolored fish hover near the corals, hide in the waving tentacles of anemones, or dart through rock crevices.

The worlds above and below the water were born in earthly tumult. Located near the juncture of two continental plates, Komodo grew from island-building volcanoes that date back 130 million years but seem to have ceased growing around 50 million years ago. Eruptions left two islands of about 300 square miles each, Komodo and Rinca, and a sprinkling of smaller ones, all between the larger Indonesian islands of Flores and Sumbawa.

The time of the construction of these islands falls well within the era when dinosaurs strode the Earth. The ancestors of monitor lizards like the Komodo dragons appeared later, though, in Central Asia about 50 million years ago. In times of lower sea levels, they moved on to Australia and the Indonesian archipelago. Rising sea levels during the end of the last ice age isolated them on these few arid, brittle Pacific islands.

Nearly rainless for six months of the year, the islands experienced little human habitation for centuries. Rusa deer, wild pigs, and water buffalo were introduced, probably as game and domestic species. More than 70 species of bird inhabited the trees, and monkeys called long-tailed macaques scampered along the ground and up into the trees. The dragons lumbered about undisturbed, and fish swarmed in the abundant coral reefs. By 1930, fewer than 50 people lived on Komodo and some 250 on Rinca.

As population pressures increased worldwide, more people began settling on the islands and boats from elsewhere began visiting the rich fishing grounds. In 1980 the Indonesian government established Komodo National Park, nearly 150,000 acres of island and ocean, mostly to preserve the unique dragons, decreasing in number as they competed for island space. By 2000, the human population had swollen to some 3,500 in Komodo National Park and perhaps 17,000 just outside its boundaries. Local food needs and market demands from distant ports were depleting fish stocks. Destructive methods of marine harvest such as blasting and cyanide poisoning were destroying the reef habitat.

In 1995 The Nature Conservancy began helping the Indonesian Ministry of Forestry protect marine resources from the impact of human activities. The ministry later asked the Conservancy to design a 25-year plan for protecting the marine systems in the park, a plan that went into effect in 2000. Stronger enforcement of laws against illegal fishing practices and the introduction of alternate sources of income may yet save an underwater treasure.

FOR DAILY GLIMPSES AT THIS WONDER WORLD, I LIVED FOR A WEEK on a hundred-foot charter boat, the *Evening Star II,* joining a half dozen divers, several of them scientists on vacation, from the United States, England, Hong Kong, and the Netherlands. Dr. Peter J. Mous, science, training, and partnerships manager for The Nature Conservancy and a specialist in fisheries management, was our host. Twice a day we roared away from the mother ship in two dinghies to choice coral reefs. Our first dive dropped us at the edge of a small island a few hundred yards from the larger Komodo. Between the two surged waters of the Indian Ocean. "If you get into the passage itself, the current will carry you away from the reefs," said our host. "So try to stay just at the edge of the current."

One by one we sat on the edge of the dinghies, held our face masks firm, and tipped backward into water of superb clarity and comfortable temperature. The boats hovered nearby to pick us up at the end of the dive, usually about an hour long. The only uncertified diver in the group, I snorkeled at and near the surface, while the others submerged to depths of 30, 60, sometimes 90 feet.

Is there any more dramatic change on Earth than moving from the atmosphere into the marine world? With the splash off the boat comes the mild shock of temperature change, subaqueous silence, and a reminder of the preciousness of air. All diminished in importance as our face masks revealed a sense of flying over a magical new realm.

The coral reef fringed the submarine rock for several dozen yards, then dropped abruptly into deeper water. The divers with tanks descended down it, expiration bubbles rising lazily to the surface. Above them I hovered face down, occasionally tipping forward in a half somersault and letting the weight of my legs drive me downward. Propelled by finned feet, I briefly shared the strange world of underwater animals anchored to the seafloor.

The building blocks for the reef are the hard corals, small colonies of animals that build calcium carbonate skeletons outside their bodies. In the larval stage they drift with the current until attaching to some stable surface where they create their limestone houses. Each polyp divides repeatedly, increasing the size of the skeleton and the colony. From within the fortress, each polyp extrudes tentacles to draw plankton into its central mouth; the tentacles draw back inside the stony structure when sensing the presence of danger.

The reef-building corals appear in irregular shapes; among them are flat table corals, some six feet across, and rounded boulder corals, some called brain corals because of the striations that make them look capable of pondering. Staghorn corals grow branches with white blossoms of tentacles reaching out from the ends. Branching corals can reproduce by division and, as the colony grows, so does the limestone they produce. When part of a branch breaks off, it may attach itself to the sea bottom and become a new colony. As individuals die, they become the substrate for more corals to build upon and thus, given enough time, coral reefs can grow into underwater mountains.

The algae that live in coral tissue create the sometimes brilliant colors and also provide nutrients for the corals. Hard corals also capture food on their own, with tentacles that contain a kind of spring-loaded dart called a nematocyst. Aside from capturing prey such as larval fish and other marine animals, the darts are fired to ward off predators. The darts of most corals can't pierce human skin but a few, like the hydroid fire coral, are best avoided.

A universe of underwater creatures in Horseshoe Bay, Rinca, includes jewel basslets schooling under a plate coral,

with damselfish joining the throng in mid-water.

Tongue flicking to taste the air, a Komodo dragon strolls at seaside in search of beached carrion.

Rising above the irregular shapes of the "stony" corals are soft corals, such as the sea fans—thin, filigreed sheets waving gently like something your traveling aunt brought home from the Orient—and sea whips, or golden spiral corals, which send a single yellow stem spiraling sometimes 10 to 15 feet up from the seafloor.

First to catch the diver's eye, however, are the anemones, their clusters of finger-like tentacles slowly moving in the ocean currents. Anemones have a body structure similar to that of corals, but no limestone skeleton supports them. Water inside their bodies keeps them from collapsing, and they undulate with a liquid grace, soft and inviting, light brown, orange, and sometimes green—also because of the symbiotic algae. The gentle appearance is deceptive, for they have stinging tentacles to catch small prey. Lurking furtively among the deadly tentacles and seemingly caressed by them are often clown fish, bright orange with white stripes.

The tubelike sponges, simple and primitive animals that existed long before corals, lend a stateliness to the seafloor. Standing in clusters of three and four, they quietly take in water through thousands of holes in their fibrous bodies, then expel it through a large hole at the top. Processing thousands of gallons of water a day, they filter out tiny plankton and bacteria for nourishment.

ACCENTING THIS SEASCAPE OF SHAPES AND COLORS is the moving, changing palette of fishes. A storm of rose-colored jewel basslets regarded me with tiny black eyes. Blue-lined surgeonfish were more businesslike, as if rushing off to the operating room in gowns of alternating blue and yellow. Butterfly fish glided by, dish-shaped in bright yellow with varying designs of deepest black. My favorite was one with masked eyes, the raccoon butterfly fish. Suddenly, below me, I spied one of the most outlandishly decorated denizens of the sea, the clown triggerfish. Arrowing down for a closer look, I saw a white back with round black spots, while its belly had the reverse—white spots on a black belly, like a clown's baggy pants. Its yellow tail waved lazily. Over a dark nose it sported a white V for good measure, and it moved unhurriedly just above the corals as if showing off its paint job.

I hauled myself back into a dinghy just before Caspar Henderson, a British journalist who had earned his scuba certification by diving in cold and murky rock quarries shortly before this trip. He emerged almost babbling from these clear, fecund waters. "My first sea dive," he gasped as soon as he had spit out his air regulator mouthpiece. "It was fantastic! I've never seen so much diversity!" With messianic zeal he relived his initiation with everyone he encountered—the Indonesian dinghy pilots, the other divers, the ship's cook.

From my companions, several of them marine biologists, came more details about the sights I'd seen. The clown fish can retreat to the safe embrace of the anemone, explained the Conservancy's Peter Mous, because it spreads mucous from the anemone all over its body, preventing the host from sensing its presence and firing the paralyzing darts. Lillian Becker, a marine biology student on fellowship with the National Marine Fisheries

Parrot fish and surgeonfish, among other reef denizens, dry on Padar Island,
in the Komodo archipelago, for sale as food. Komodo National Park allows some legal fishing,
but poachers harvesting with homemade bombs damage coral communities.

Service, pointed out that stony corals reproduce not only by division but also by annual mass spawnings that release sperm and eggs, which become the drifting larvae.

From Yvonne Sadovy, a marine biologist at the University of Hong Kong, came a strange tale of sexual metamorphosis among my favorite fish, the jewel basslets. If a shortage of males occurs among these rose-colored gems, the largest of the females undergoes a self-induced sex change. The switch in behavior happens almost immediately: The fish becomes more aggressive and helps defend the territory against other species of similar size. Over a couple of weeks, the organs follow suit, changing from female to male.

AFTER LUNCH AND A SHORT REST WE BOARDED THE DINGHIES for our second dive of the day. A long-ago eruption had built up lava from the seafloor, a construction known as a seamount. Only a few square feet of rock pierced the ocean surface, but the slopes underwater were blanketed by corals, anemones, and sponges and patrolled by fish. Peter suggested we stay on the leeward side of the rock to avoid fighting to stay in place. These same currents, of course, enrich the reefs with a constant smorgasbord of microscopic life and can give divers a look at sea life on both ends of the spectrum. Indonesia is the world's only equatorial region where gaps between landmasses allow the exchange of plants and animals between oceans. One of those passages is through the Komodo archipelago, a migration route for blue, sperm, and minke whales. Unfortunately, none showed up during our stay.

Below the surface did appear an ever changing parade of smaller fish. Two black and white dish-shaped characters glided by, white banners waving garishly up and over their backs—Moorish idols. Challenging the jewel basslets of the first dive for beauty honors were yellowtail blue damselfish, bodies gleaming like sapphires. Far below me I saw a flash of pure butter color, and I dove to see a yellow chromis, slightly larger than my hand, nibbling along the slope. The most frequently seen nibblers, parrotfish of iridescent green, appeared on every dive, grinding at dead coral with their buck teeth to eat algae and sea worms.

Several times we broke from diving to hike on the islands, where my introduction to the Komodo dragons fell short of fearsome expectations. Half expecting to see villagers terrorized by the famous lizards, I was disappointed to see my first of the scaly reptiles spread like sleeping dogs under one of the raised rattan huts. Villagers maintain a safe distance from the dragons, which would never qualify as pets. These lizards have learned that aggressive moves toward people will be repulsed by a long, forked stick. Two dragons lay under an empty schoolhouse, making recess a dicey prospect. Off by himself sprawled the biggest of them, a hulking, nine-foot dragon of especially bad temper which the villagers named *Awas!*—Watch Out! Quarrels with others of his kind had torn off a corner of his mouth and left him with a sneering look of special malevolence.

An uneasy truce exists. These dragons allow tourists to approach within a dozen feet to photograph them lying somnolently in the dust. Move too close, though, and they raise their heads, flick out long, forked, satanic tongues, and hiss and rumble ominous warnings.

From the mouths of some pour streams of drool, as if imagining you sliding down their fetid gullet. Instead of breathing fire, these dragons expel a world-class halitosis caused by massive amounts of bacteria in their tooth-lined mouths. The dragon young, after hatching from eggs buried in the sand, live their first months in trees—to avoid being eaten by their parents or other adults of their kind. Compared to Komodo dragons, crocodiles seem almost amiable.

Acclimated though the village dragons may be toward people, a walk in the Komodo countryside would be ill advised without a local guide. Dragons strike from ambush, lying beside trails to wait for prey to pass by. After a quick rush and a savage bite—with a mouth lined with daggerlike teeth—to the hindquarters of a deer, water buffalo, wild pig, or horse, a Komodo dragon retreats with reptilian patience. The bacteria-laden bite causes severe infection, and the victim soon dies of blood poisoning within a week. The smell of carrion in the tropical sun draws other dragons to dine. Two of our party were sea kayaking along the shore one day and saw three dragons devouring a deer on the beach. They described the hissing controversy and savage rending of flesh as a scene from prehistory.

We saw no dragons during a trail walk on Komodo, only the large burrows they dig as retreats in the heat of the day. Deer peered at us through veils of brush before bounding over the low hills. Wild pigs trotted away on incredibly lean shanks. Macaques sat in the dust to watch us with expressive eyes, always moving back a safe distance when we came too close. Overhead, sulfur-crested cockatoos razzed and scolded us. Something moved on a tree as we passed by, and our guide snatched it to show us a small "flying" lizard. A spread of skin between front legs and body opens like a fan to let it glide to safety when hotly pursued.

Strolling in the heat of the day among thirsty trees and through brittle grasses, we finally sighted dragons in the wild. One lay in the shade of a palm tree and looked incapable of stirring. We walked on, past wild water buffalo that eyed us impassively from mud wallows they had hollowed out of a barely trickling stream. Descending a hill, we came to a ravine, and our guide, a local man named Manuel, turned right a few yards for a detour around a damp seep. I considered taking a shortcut but instead followed him—fortunately. As we came around the far side of the ravine, a lively dragon crawled out the opposite bank. No noon sleeper, it held its head erect, flicked out its tongue to taste the air, and turned its head to consider us. It is a strange feeling to have a creature regard you with gastronomic interest. This one apparently decided we were not worth a lunge across a ravine in the hot sun, or perhaps remembered having its nose pushed into the dirt by a forked stick.

We never felt in danger, but I asked Manuel if his stick would truly stop a charging dragon. He assured me that it would. I asked him if it would stop two charging dragons. He didn't answer and walked on.

DESPITE THEIR ARIDITY, THESE ISLANDS POSSESS A STARK BEAUTY. From the sea they appear tan and barren, although our walks showed them to be covered with grasses that seem to sustain the grazers in the dry months from May to October. Often, as we leaned

Aerial view shows a mangrove-skirted lagoon and coral reefs along the northwest shore of Rinca Island.
Reefs parallel the coastline just offshore, showing up as pale green.
Like the island's mountains themselves, the ocean floor slopes steeply, showing here as deep blue.

on the rail of the *Evening Star II,* nursing a cold beer in the fading light, we saw Rusa deer strolling and nipping at something obscurely edible.

One night we were moving to the site of the next morning's dive, and a bevy of porpoises accompanied us, plunging just ahead of the prow and clearing the water in syrupy leaps. Their surging bodies stirred tiny bioluminescent creatures in the seawater into brief, bright shows of phosphorescence, making the porpoises appear to trail streaks of white fire.

Winking at night like stars in the dark water were many lanterns of the island fishermen. Their small boats bobbed gently in the quiet waters, long extensions off each side to net squid, anchovies, and sardines. A zoning system within park boundaries allows some traditional fishing while protecting other valuable and sensitive locations. Other legal fishing methods include gill nets, hooks and lines, trolling, and capturing live fish with traps made of bamboo. Most fishermen catch herringlike small fish for sale as cheap protein or even chicken feed. Parrrotfish and surgeonfish are dried, salted, and sold as food to other islands.

Any type of fishing can tax resources, but of special concern in the archipelago are blast fishing and cyanide poisoning, techniques used mostly by renegade outsiders from distant islands. Blasting dates back to World War II, when local fishermen observed that after an explosion in the water, a large amount of reef fish floated up: easy pickings. When leftover bombs ran out, they began making their own out of chemical fertilizers.

Handmade bombs usually mean a beer bottle containing a mixture of kerosene and ammonium nitrate, ignited by a fuse. Blasters first locate a school of fish around a reef by looking underwater with goggles or a face mask. They light the fuse and toss the bomb into the school, then, after the explosion, they enter the water to collect the commercial species stunned or killed by the shock wave. Everything dies within a diameter of at least 15 feet—invertebrates, sponges, basslets, damselfish—in addition to the saleable species. The corals are blown into rubble. Several times in my dives over living, moving communities of brilliant color, I drifted into areas blasted dead as a boneyard, where shards of limestone and broken arms of staghorn coral littered a barren seafloor.

Half the reefs in the Komodo area show some damage caused by blast fishing, says Helen Fox, a University of California researcher who surveys the waters with a grant from The Nature Conservancy. "Recovery is slow because the coral larvae need a stable surface on which to establish themselves, and the rubble moves around in the current," she told us one night on the *Evening Star II.* "It could take 40 to 70 years for natural recovery of the reef, and centuries for it to return to what it once was." Dumping boulders into a blasted area seems to speed the process, she says, giving the coral larvae something stable to settle on.

While divers from the developed world feel outrage at coral destruction, island fishermen need an income. We beached our dinghies at the fishing village on Komodo Island and were immediately surrounded by troops of bright-faced children and adults with quick, warm smiles. Their houses appeared solid, and through some doors gleamed television images.

We were invited into the house of Ishaka, a former pearl diver who now carves wooden dragons and makes pearl necklaces. Tourism has made him the wealthiest man in the village, and he misses pearl diving not at all. Others have followed his course. From three different vendors I bought necklaces of both black and white pearls at very reasonable prices and an excellent carved wooden dragon that now glares from my living room mantle.

Despite the ready smiles of the villagers, the quality of life here is poor. Unclean water in the dry season brings widespread illness, and the few medical clinics are poorly equipped. Often water for consumption must be boated in from elsewhere in jerry cans. Extreme aridity makes agriculture impossible, and 97 percent of the islands' income comes from fishing. The catch, highly perishable in the tropical sun, must be quickly salted and dried, and in that condition it brings a low price. Live fish command a much higher price.

Serving a large, freshly killed fish has become a status symbol among the nouveau riche of Hong Kong and southern China, and a lucrative business of delivering live fish to those areas has developed. Yvonne Sadovy, who has studied the trade, told me over dinner on the *Evening Star II* that one live fish more than six feet long sold for $10,000 in Hong Kong. Ships with water-circulating holding tanks have been built by traders to keep the catch alive on the way to market. Only a fraction of the profits trickles down to the fisherman, but trade in still living fish remains attractive to a family that must buy water to drink.

Capturing live fish with cyanide is much quicker than waiting for them to enter a homemade bamboo trap. Cyanide fishermen descend to a reef using a primitive diving device called a hookah, which supplies air through hoses from a compressor on a boat. Sighting large fish such as grouper, sea bass, coral trout, or Napoleon wrasse, they chase their prey into a coral hiding place and then squirt in cyanide diluted with water. The mixture temporarily paralyzes the fish, then the diver tears away the coral with an iron bar to capture the drugged creature and slowly escort it to the boat above. Divers also capture spiny lobsters for the live trade in Bali and Java. To gather large numbers of colorful, small fish for aquariums, cyanide is sprayed over a wide area, resulting in high mortality. Corals die from the cyanide and from being pried loose in the collection of the poisoned catch.

Blasting, cyanide use, and overfishing have all brought a decline in fish stocks to Komodo National Park. "Grouper, for example, gather in large swarms to reproduce," explained Yvonne, "and fishermen find these sites and collect them. So the large aggregations for reproduction are happening less and less, because there are simply fewer fish."

To protect the dwindling resource, the Conservancy recommends monitoring fishing boats and reef ecology and introducing new fish-gathering methods. Government boats now patrol the waters to enforce regulations, but the oceans are huge and the island channels a maze. Mooring buoys sunk into the ocean floor prevent damage from the anchors of boats. The Nature Conservancy has also encouraged the taking of larger fish from deeper waters—pelagic fishing—to steer fishermen away from the reefs. A series of rafts have been anchored far offshore to attract deepwater fish that like to collect under floating objects and to make those fish more accessible to the boatmen. "We don't know why fish gather under them," said Peter Mous, "but they do. I saw one rubbing against the raft once, so maybe when the ocean floor is a mile below, they simply want something to scratch on."

Mariculture, or fish farming, may offer an alternative to cyanide fishing for the live fish trade. Villagers will raise fish in underwater cages just outside park boundaries, beginning with wild-caught grouper, barramundi, and snapper species and raising subsequent generations to maturity for commercial sale. As of 2002, 200 groupers and a total of 130 mangrove snappers and barramundi were being tended as brood stock for the planned hatchery.

Uneducated fishermen are becoming aware of the value of live reefs, although most of them still refer to the corals as rocks, said Peter. "There are still poachers who fish illegally, who use cyanide and explosives, and who go ashore with spotlights and kill deer, but they are reckless cowboys. Most people now try to follow regulations."

Preservation of the beauty of the reefs also means increased income to the locals through tourism. More than 30,000 tourists, 90 percent of them international visitors, now come annually to the Komodo archipelago to view the underwater scenes. Besides diving, they visit the dragon habitats, paying guides and buying carvings, necklaces, and bracelets made by villagers. Entrance fees to areas where dragons can be seen have been raised from the equivalent of two dollars to twenty.

OUR DIVING SITES ESCALATED IN BEAUTY as the week progressed. We moved to the southern reaches of the park, where cold water surged from the deep sea, bringing a cornucopia of nutrients to feed reefs of amazing color and variety.

In a rain forest one pushes through underbrush in sticky heat, peering for colorful birds and butterflies, pleased at a troop of monkeys, exulting at a large mammal. In a rich coral reef, though, you join the wildlife in their own multihued world. Small fish crowd close to peer into the one oval eye of the ungainly newcomer. Larger fish size you up casually from a short distance, sensing that you are incapable of hot pursuit. A manta ray may pass over like a dark cloud, a gentle wave from one broad wing nearly knocking off your face mask. A green sea turtle as big as a coffee table swoops away from you with strong thrusts of its flippers.

On our final day, the deep divers joined me in snorkeling, since they needed to decompress for the plane ride to Bali the following day. We rode the current through passages between islands, scanning the ever changing panoply below. I saw many old friends. Moorish idols paraded by, banners waving. Clown fish hovered among the anemones. Surgeonfish rushed off to appointments. Sea fans waved a slow good-bye.

Finally, I saw an entire school of fish completely new to me. Hundreds of handsized blue fusiliers, sky-colored except for a spot of black at the very tips of their tails, passed slowly before me like a lazy, wavering curtain, like a pale, pleasant dream that drifts across your brain just before you awake refreshed. A dream seemed an appropriate way to end a visit to a fairyland. I turned back to the world of air and heaved myself over the side of the dinghy. ■

pacific
islands
portfolio

∿

ELABORATE CENTERPIECE for a coral reef, a colony of
red whip gorgonians rises amid large plates
of cabbage coral in Kimbe Bay, Papua New Guinea.
In the Pacific, underwater corals and islands above
offer gardens of visual delights, now often
sullied by human carelessness.

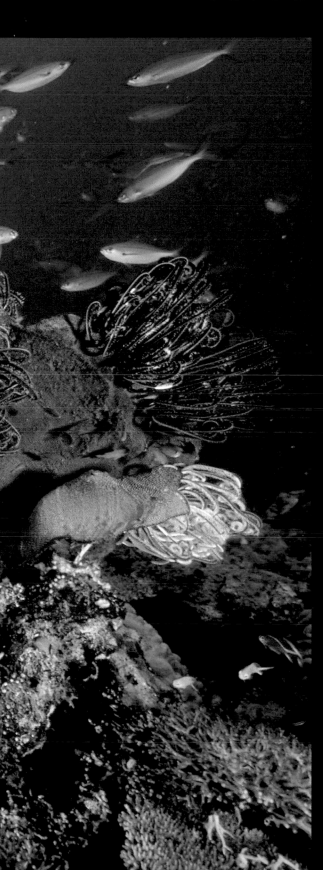

SILVERY FUSILIERS stream by elephant's ear sponges festooned with crinoids— reef animals with feathery arms—at Kimbe Bay. Where rich, tropical waters of the western Pacific touch Papua New Guinea's densely forested island of New Britain, nutrients from both land and sea feed an astounding variety of marine life. A biological inventory of the bay revealed 320 species of coral and 800 species of reef fish.

Runoff from heavily logged areas and the use of explosives in fishing now threaten these magnificent reefs. To combat destruction, The Nature Conservancy helped develop a nongovernmental organization called Mahonia na Dari (Guardian of the Sea), which promotes conservation programs in the Papua New Guinea education system. A new conservation and research center trains high school students in marine biology, education, agriculture, and ecoforestry, so they might spread conservation to New Britain villages.

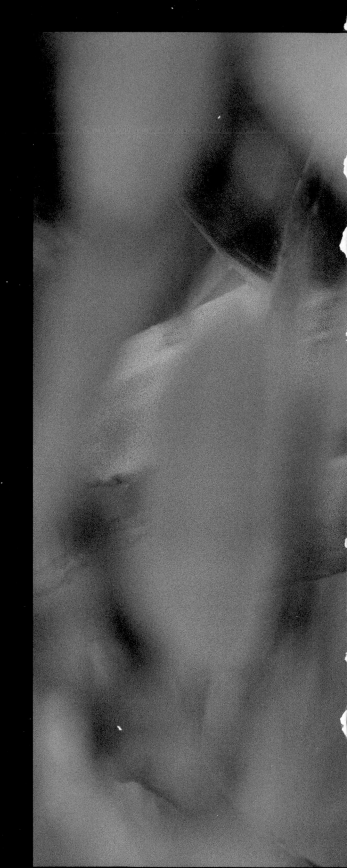

PROUD PROFILE of the red-knobbed
hornbill decorates the rain forests of Lore
Lindu National Park on Indonesia's island
of Sulawesi. The huge beak and brilliant
feathers can also be its downfall, as native
hunters seek the large bird for food or
decoration. A third of the 227 bird species
in this half-million-acre park are found
nowhere else. More than half the island's
species of mammals also exist only on
Sulawesi and in Lore Lindu, including the
dwarf buffalo; the world's smallest pri-
mate, the tarsier; and the babirusa, an
animal resembling both pig and hippo-
potamus, with two sets of curling tusks.

Working with Indonesian park
authorities, The Nature Conservancy
tries to raise conservation awareness
through education programs and training
and by instilling locals with pride in their
irreplaceable creatures. Ecological
enterprises such as sustainable agriculture, honey collecting, and ecotourism
are being introduced.

AMOEBALIKE SHAPES 600 miles east of the Philippines shelter what scientists and divers call one of the Seven Underwater Wonders of the World. The 350 jungled islands of the Republic of Palau are former coral reefs heaved above sea level millions of years ago by volcanic pressure. Three ocean currents converge on the tightly bunched archipelago, nurturing an unrivaled diversity of marine life. The waters support 350 species of hard and soft corals and some 1,400 species of reef fish. Endangered and vulnerable species— dugong (related to the manatee), saltwater crocodile, hawksbill and green sea turtles— also live here.

Economic pressures of tourism and fishing threaten the local ecology. To encourage conservation and counter the effects of a 52-mile paved road being built around the largest island, Babeldaob, the Conservancy works with local officials on the responsible use of land and marine resources and guards against illegal fishing.

A GREY REEF SHARK pauses before another gulping dash into a large mass of baitfish near one of the Arnavon Islands in the Solomons. Plentiful marine resources once marked this double chain of 922 islands east of Papua New Guinea. An exploding human population now taxes the environment. Overharvesting threatens the hawksbill turtle and its eggs in one of the world's most important rookeries for the endangered sea turtle. At the invitation of three villages and in partnership with the Solomon Islands government, the Conservancy helped establish the Arnavon Islands Marine Conservation Area to allow resources to recover. The program may be expanded to other islands.

ROBELIKE COLORS and a smug look gave the splendid mandarin fish its name.

SPECTERS FRINGED with fuzz, an Irish setter ghost pupfish eyes the photographer warily

LOOKING LIKE a Lilliputian at work, entomologist Steve Montgomery collects insects among umbrella-like leaves of the 'ape plant, sometimes three feet wide atop four-foot stems. Hundreds of native Hawaiian species of plants, birds, and insects, many of them endangered or rare, live in the Waikamoi Preserve on the island of Maui. Owned by the Haleakala Ranch, the 5,230-acre sanctuary is managed by The Nature Conservancy and the state. The mat of greenery represents a small part of the 100,000-acre East Maui Watershed, which provides 60 billion gallons of clean water annually to Maui residents, businesses, and farmers. To ensure its flow into the future, The Nature Conservancy, the ranch, and state officials cooperate in protecting some of the best remaining forest in Hawai'i.

UNRAVELING THE mysteries of life in the
Kamakou Preserve, a *hapu'u* fiddlehead
(right) stretches out into a frond of the
tree fern. The branches of a small club
moss, called *lepelepe-a-moa* in Hawaiian
(far right), are often woven with
rosebuds into leis.

A 2,774-acre rain forest near the top of
the highest mountain on Moloka'i,
Kamakou presents a unique biology. Of
Hawai'i's 250 plant species, 219 are found
nowhere else on Earth and attract
unusual insects and birds that feed on
them. Marooned thousands of miles from
any other landmass, life in the islands of
Hawai'i adapted into specialized forms.
Introduced species now compete for
space and resources, so that Hawai'i has
lost more adapted species than all of
North America. To prevent further losses,
The Nature Conservancy and government
agencies now manage Kamakou Preserve,
protecting native species and educating
the public.

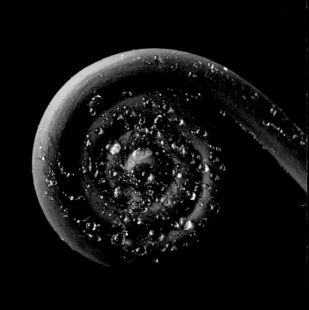

CENTRAL AND SOUTH

AMERICA

A quetzal, sacred to the ancient Maya,
peers from its nest in Guatemala.
Habitat destruction now threatens its existence.

Planets align over a temple at Guatemala's Tikal, a restored city of the ancient Maya.

lost worlds, lush edens

∾

If the ancient Maya had been as concerned about
forests as one of their descendants, their
widespread civilization might have endured.
"I love the trees, and I hate to see them
disappear," said Nazario Ku, a burly,
full-blooded Maya who lives in northern Belize.
"My father used to ask a tree's forgiveness
every time he cut one down."

WHETHER THEY APOLOGIZED OR NOT, the Maya of the first millennium leveled much of the lush rain forest of Central America. From A.D. 250 to 900 they terraced hillsides, dug canals, and filled marshy areas to feed one of the first truly complex societies in the New World, in a region anthropologists refer to culturally as Mesoamerica. Maya art and intellectual accomplishments were comparable to those of ancient capitals in Asia and Africa. The sudden collapse of their civilization, archaeologists now believe, may have stemmed from a large and demanding population depleting the bared soils.

By the time Spaniards viewed the remnants of Maya cities in the early 1500s, the great rain forests had already reestablished themselves. Today a green belt extends across the slim waist of the Americas, nurtured by bountiful rains that come between May and October. The result is vegetation run riot, masses of growth from the forest floor to the crowns of trees more than one hundred feet high. From the air, the Central American rain forest can be seen stretching to the horizon—a leafy, unbroken ocean swimming with life. Within it, and in forests similar to it around the world, live at least a third of all the species on Earth.

Prowling the jungled floor of Belize and Guatemala are muscular jaguars and smaller felines such as the ocelot and jaguarundi. Howler and spider monkeys swing from the treetops and drink carefully from the many streams where crocodiles dwell. Hundreds of species of birds row the air, and millions of insects own the night. On a single acre of rain forest ground, there may be ten times the number of tree species as might be found in the eastern deciduous forest near my home in Virginia. Many smaller plants have never been identified and catalogued.

That splendid green belt with its galaxy of life is once again being thinned by modern farmers and loggers in a growing population. The losses this time may affect not only Central America but also societies worldwide. Climatologists now see the forests as huge producers of oxygen and huge sinks for the increasing amounts of carbon dioxide in Earth's atmosphere. Biologists say destruction of rain forests causes massive extinctions, and only a handful of the species that live in them have been tested for possible medicinal use. Ornithologists know that many songbirds seen in North America in summer spend their winters in the forests of Central America.

Birds still sing and carbon still sinks into large tracts of forest in Belize, thanks to efforts of the leading environmental organization in the country, called Programme for Belize (PFB). The group, based in Belize City, receives financial and technical support from The Nature Conservancy. Working together, the two organizations have set aside by purchase and through donation nearly 250,000 acres of rain forest, now managed by PFB.

The lands acquired have checkered histories. Some were logged for mahogany and cedar by a Belizean company in the early 1900s. Most were crisscrossed by private *chicleros,* workers who slashed the bark of sapodilla trees to gather chicle sap for use in chewing gum, killing some trees in the process. Coca-Cola bought large tracts for citrus groves but abandoned those plans and sold and donated land to save songbird habitat. Utility companies in the United States and Canada also donated land, anticipating that world agreements might allow them to build up "carbon credits"—saving carbon dioxide–eating forests to offset the carbon dioxide released by their facilities.

The combined lands now totally owned by Programme for Belize comprise a thick swath of forest known as the Rio Bravo Conservation and Management Area. In Guatemala, huge tracts have been set aside as national parks and reserves. For weeks I traveled the rivers, roads, and forest trails of the two countries with people on the front lines in the battle to save rain forests. Part of that battle includes teaching local people how to live productively with a forest, and making them aware of the treasure that could be lost along with the big trees.

ONE WHO DIDN'T NEED MUCH CONVINCING was the tree lover Nazario Ku, who believes forests and people can coexist. A modern Maya whose shining black hair hangs in a ponytail down his broad back, Nazario works as a caretaker at the nearby Lamani archaeological site, an ancient Maya complex near his home in the village of Chunox. He partners with five neighbors in tending hives of bees that make honey from the many flowers of the forest. They first sold it locally in recycled rum bottles, but now they put it in squeeze tubes and open-necked jars for city markets. Nazario also raises butterflies, to give them a better chance at survival in a shrinking habitat.

He opened the door to a screened-in enclosure near his house and invited me into a lush garden. Morpho butterflies of beautiful blue fluttered from one green plant to another. Sipping sugary juices from a bowl of sliced fruit were two owl butterflies, named for the large spots on their wings that look like the eyes of a large bird and may deter enemies. Smaller long-wing butterflies known as zebras, postmen, and Isabellas also flitted about the winged zoo.

Nazario lifted a broad leaf to reveal butterfly eggs on the underside. When the eggs hatch, he moves the larvae to another hut, a screened nursery where they pupate without being attacked by parasitic wasps. "See, here is one that has recently emerged," he said, touching a broad-winged beauty still perched on its cocoon. As if acknowledging its benefactor, the butterfly's first wing beats propelled it to Nazario's forehead. Unmoving, he added, "When they have flown enough in here to grow strong, I open the door and let them out.

"In the three years I have been doing this, I have released perhaps 10,000," he said. "They are having a tough time, losing habitat to man and being attacked by parasitic wasps and birds, so I try to give them a head start." Nazario invites schoolchildren to his house to see the butterfly garden, hoping to raise their environmental consciences. The garden was his own idea, but the bee project was proposed by Programme for Belize.

PFB worker Ramon Pacheco, a handsome, young, mustachioed Belizean, picked me up when I arrived at Belize City airport and drove me to La Milpa field station, which he manages as part of the Rio Bravo project. In the Maya language, *la milpa* means "cornfield," and the two-acre clearing was a small farm a decade ago. By replacing corn with grass and a homesteader's hut with solid thatched cabanas and a colorful hardwood dormitory, PFB created a rustic campus. From April through August, high school and university students and teachers from the United States, Canada, and Belize come for short

Fairyland forest in the clouds, the Sierra de las Minas Biosphere Reserve in Guatemala spans elevations from 50 to 10,000

feet, prime habitat for threatened quetzals.

Hanging heliconias dangle like half-boiled lobster claws in a Belizean rain forest, nursery as well to orchids, begonias,

philodendrons, and other brilliant flowers.

courses in ecology, walking jungle trails while instructors talk about the plants and animals that live there. "We hope they all go home with enthusiastic stories about the rain forest and why it should be saved," said Ramon, a former high school teacher now at La Milpa.

What a classroom! I awoke each morning under my mosquito netting to an alarm clock of birdsong and rose to see wild oscillated turkeys and deer feeding on the station's lawn. Walks in the forest with La Milpa naturalist Bladmir Rodriguez were filled with details of life in the green maze. He pointed out the curved thorns of the bullhorn acacia, a low tree that has a symbiotic relationship with its small tenants. Stinging ants live among the thorns and discourage animals from eating the plant. In return, the ants dine on a yellow material produced in new leaf growth. If bitten by a snake, Bladmir pointed out, you can tear off an arm's-length strip of the tree's bark, chew it, swallow the juice, and apply the chewed bark on the wound as a poultice.

I asked about a golf ball–size hole in the ground. Bladmir plucked a long blade of grass and inserted it into the hole, wiggling it provocatively as he slowly pulled it out again. Out lunged a dark, hairy tarantula, who thought the blade the antennae of an insect invading its lair. Fierce-looking and capable of a painful, stabbing bite, the big spider is harmless if not provoked.

We passed a cahune palm, which has a soft edible heart. Its leaves are used for thatching huts, and its nuts can be burned like coal or boiled down to produce cooking oil. The best leaves for thatch, however, come from young sabal palms, which offer a sustainable income from the forest. Some tourist resorts seeking a tropical motif now offer the equivalent of 50 cents per leaf. "Your cabana would require about 8,000," said Bladmir, "but the gatherers must not be too greedy. If they take more than two from a single young plant, it will die."

We saw sapodilla trees with the V-shaped slashes that mark the work of chicleros draining the sap, known as chicle, for chewing gum. Death of a sapodilla from too many wounds removes one of the hardest trees in the forest. Its wood makes durable handles for axes and hammers, and beams carved from it by the ancient Maya a thousand years ago still buttress doorways in ruined palaces.

We gave wide berth to a poisonwood tree, since contact with it raises blisters much worse than poison ivy. For every problem in the forest there seems to be a solution: If afflicted by poisonwood, a cut in the gumbo limbo tree yields sap that eases the itching.

So many plants of the forest are used by native Belizeans that Bladmir guided me another day on a stroll that he called "the medicine walk." Although few of the remedies he showed me carry the validation of medical research, forest dwellers use them regularly. "Here's coriander," he said, pointing to a vine growing close to the ground. "People flavor food with it, but it also settles an upset stomach.

"Hog plum," he continued, pointing to a low shrub. "Boil its bark and the buds of its flowers for ten minutes, and it helps cure a sore throat or diarrhea." Native women had long boiled the otherwise inedible wild yam to make a tea that worked as a contraceptive. Now, it has become an important source for female progesterone in contraceptive pills. "Men also use its strong vine as rope," Bladmir added.

A camera trap captures a male jaguar patrolling his territory in Belize, site of the world's first jaguar sanctuary. Despite a shrinking habitat, the largest cat in the Americas holds strong in large forested enclaves, making it less threatened than most big cats of the world.

On and on. The juice of chinaroot, boiled and mixed with condensed milk, tastes like Ovaltine and gives you energy. Breadnut resin, applied to an aching tooth, loosens it so you can pull it yourself. Boiled trumpet tree leaves cure both low blood pressure and diabetes. From a massive giant with spreading branches and the unglamorous name of stinking toe tree comes a seed said to be high in iron and therefore good for anemia—if you can get past the aroma of unwashed feet.

"IT'S A JUNGLE OUT THERE," GOES THE SAYING, suggesting a place of treachery and hardship where danger lurks behind every leaf and tree trunk. I have known instead in the rain forest a rich world filled with fascinating species and deep quiet. A policy of live and let live seems to reign, except where hunger intervenes. Humans are food for very few except a myriad of bugs, and modern potions mostly keep them at bay. Snakes hide or flee except when provoked. The furtive jaguar and forest puma avoid us and are rarely seen. Even crocodiles splash away in panic at our approach. We are the most dangerous animal in the jungle.

The dangers are there for the unwary, just as they are on a crowded, high-speed freeway. I would never swim in a crocodile stream and let myself be mistaken for a river-crossing tapir. As we passed a cahune palm, Bladmir pointed to the litter at its base and cautioned about snakes. "Never walk through the dead fronds or disturb them," he said. "The fer-de-lance loves to hide there and, if disturbed, its bite is deadly."

Approached with reasonable vigilance, though, an intriguing Eden awaits. The dank smell of vegetation fills the nose as the profusion of life fills the eyes. A sense of returning to the dawn of time prevails. In morning and evening, birds fill the air with the sounds of joy, perhaps delighted that they survived the night.

Before breakfast, and before the heat of the day drove birds to silence in cooler interiors of the forest, I often walked La Milpa's edges with Bladmir, an accomplished spotter. On the first morning he put his powerful scope on a pair of toucans on the far side of the clearing, and their brightly colored, oversize bills jumped to within yards of me. Shifting the scope slightly to the left, he showed me two green Aztec parakeets. We walked a few steps and he scoped a lineated woodpecker with a brilliant red crest flaring above its head.

We saw many species in a huge stinking toe tree, a popular bird tenement. The ruckus created by a pair of brown jays made them easy to spot. We also spied a smaller relative of the toucan called the collared aracari, as well as a roadside hawk, a dot-winged antwren, and a black-headed trogon. Bladmir's sharp eyes picked out a tiny but colorful green flycatcher. He confessed he could not differentiate it from the many other similar flycatchers unless it sang—which it didn't.

Its strains might have told of an incredible odyssey. Surveys have shown that of the 337 different species of birds using the Rio Bravo project area, 62 migrate from North America to winter there, then return north in spring to hatch their eggs. More types of migratory birds winter in the former British colony than in any other Central American country. "Without the forest," said Ramon, who joined us at midwalk, "many of those birds might eventually disappear."

Gone would be the indigo bunting, as lovely a flash of blue as one can see among the leaves. Gone too would be the flaming patches on the American redstart and the orange splash of the Baltimore oriole. Stilled would be choirs of warblers that ply their tiny wings all the way to Belize to escape the northern cold.

Recognizing the plight of migratory birds, The Nature Conservancy has nurtured a partnership between the Rio Bravo area and its own Edge of Appalachia Preserve in southern Ohio, where many of the birds spend their summers. With the linkage comes a shared commitment to bird conservation, exchange visits, and the exchange of ideas about managing bird habitats. Programme for Belize also subscribes to the Meso-American Biological Corridor Program, a plan funded by the World Bank to create continuous forested lanes through Central America.

Another well-used bird roost in La Milpa was a kapok tree, a smooth-trunked giant towering above the others. "The ancient Maya considered it sacred," explained Ramon, "because they felt its root system represented the afterlife; its straight, nearly branchless trunk represented the middle world where people lived; and its broad crown represented the upper world of the gods."

SIXTY MAYA SITES HAVE BEEN FOUND on Rio Bravo land, some 1,200 in all Belize. Not far from La Milpa can be found a multitiered complex of once grand palaces and temples, now crumbling and crawling with vines and shrubs. Trees grow out of altars where prisoners collected in Maya wars were sacrificed to the gods. A raccoonlike coatimundi, browsing for insects, strolled through the ruined ball court where Maya athletes played games that represented struggles between good and evil. The overgrown splendor reminded me of the poem by Percy Bysshe Shelley about the traveler who comes across a statue half-buried in a desert on which are written the words: "My name is Ozymandias, king of kings: Look on my works, ye Mighty, and despair!"

Ramon Pacheco walked me over a courtyard once paved with hardened marl, now covered with the trees and leaf litter of a thousand years. Around it stood the long stone palaces with vaulted ceilings where the elite lived. Near the center of the plaza gaped a man-made cavern, which I entered cautiously, mindful that snakes might find it an agreeable hangout. Sides that had not crumbled were shaped like an inverted funnel, and the original entrance was through a single manhole at the top. It was a storage pit, where perishable foods were kept in cool temperatures. In the dim light, the soft wing of a bat brushed my cheek and spooked me into retreat.

Back on the plaza, I imagined long-ago throngs of humanity with confident rulers, elegant women, successful traders, and darting, laughing children. I climbed to the peak of the main temple and looked down on the tops of trees. In ancient times I would have

Rock stair steps churn water into a froth as the Busilja River empties into the Usumacinta River,
which divides Mexico and Guatemala. On the Guatemalan bank, to the northeast of the river, lies
the half-million-acre wilderness of the Sierra del Lacandon National Park. Southwest of the river,
Mexican farmers have removed much natural cover in slash-and-burn agriculture.

been looking down at the terraced croplands and huts of commoners. "Some 40,000 people may have lived in the central complex and its suburbs," said Ramon, "but it was abandoned quite suddenly. Perhaps when the lands were depleted and famine came, the common people rose up against the elite." Other theories suggest that constant warfare brought about the civilization's collapse. "One to two million people lived in what is now Belize at the time of the Maya," Ramon continued. "The forests were about 80 percent cleared. Now the population is about 250,000"—and growing, threatening a last great stronghold of biology. When the Maya thinned the Central American forests in the first millennium, vast forests still existed near the Equator in other parts of the world. Now all shrink in the face of demands for lumber and croplands.

A MAJOR THREAT TO THE FOREST in Belize is posed by a people known more for peacefulness than plundering. Bordering the Rio Bravo are properties owned by Mennonites, lured from Mexico to Belize with land grants in the 1950s because of their reputations as efficient farmers. Grown prosperous, they buy more land as it becomes available, then bulldoze it into pastures and fields. Mennonite production of beans and irrigated rice has made Belize self-sufficient in these national foods. One Mennonite community produces 90 percent of the nation's sorghum.

A quiet tension exists between the religious group and their Belizean neighbors. The natives resent the gobbling of land and destruction of forests by the outsiders. Recently, a fire ignited to burn off crop residue jumped into the Rio Bravo forest and scorched thousands of acres. The Mennonites, though they lift a friendly wave to everyone they pass on the rough roads, maintain their own stores, school their own children, and forbid marriage between their own kind and native Belizeans.

While the Mennonites and others convert the forest for new uses, Programme for Belize experiments with ways to use the forest without destroying it. In the village of San Lazaro, they lend assistance to a small group trying to rebuild it.

In the stupefying noon heat, members of the Rio Hondo Environmental Conservation Organization led me into a little park and to the shade of a giant guanacaste tree, where we sat on stumps chainsawed into chairs. "We hear the news like everybody else, that forests around the world are being destroyed," said Francisco Tillett, one of these seven men and four women who vowed they wouldn't let that happen in Belize. "Much of our forest has been turned into savannas, and we're trying to learn how to convert them back again."

Near us, sprouts of mahogany and cedar poked out of the ground, along with saplings of mango, cashew, orange, and sapodilla trees. A small nursery grows seedlings for more plantings. The little park is a model of what this group plans on a larger scale, rebuilding forests and gaining income by the careful, sustainable harvest of timber and food crops. They have leased 200 acres to expand their experiment, and already some local farmers are planting trees as well. "The food is also there for the birds, as part of the biological corridor Central Americans are trying to establish," said Francisco. "We think there will be enough for both people and wildlife."

Several hours away, seven villages along the Belize River have combined their efforts to save forests and redirect their lives in the process. The grassroots aim of the BELRIV Project, also encouraged by Programme for Belize, is to lift the villages out of poverty by resurrecting income from the land. Twelve landowners agreed to spare their contiguous forests to create habitat for a troop of howler monkeys, and tourists now pay an entrance fee and hire guides to visit the sanctuary. Wives gather jungle fruits and make jams and jellies to sell. One man makes alcoholic drinks from rain forest products and sells them in his bar.

The typical congenial and burly bartender, Charles Belgrove leaned on his elbows over the counter and asked what I'd like to try. I sipped at wines made from cassava, wild berries, cedar bark, and cocoa plum, but the biggest hit was a potion made from the seeds of my old friend, the stinking toe tree. Champagne it was not but it was pleasant tasting, and fermentation had killed the smell of dirty feet. Charles mixed it with condensed milk, a concoction as satisfying as fortified eggnog, and one which he insisted enriches the blood. Medicinal booze from the rain forest.

Ramon drove me to Hill Bank, the second field station in Rio Bravo, also an educational campus for visiting students. It sits on the banks of the New River Lagoon and was formerly a base for lumber extraction. Logs dragged from the forest and then hauled there on narrow-gauge railways were dumped into the lagoon and floated to sawmills at Belize City and Orange Walk. The once busy lumber camp now serves as a base for saving the rain forest, not destroying it.

Preservation requires money to support field stations, equipment, and workers, and PFB struggles to create income flow. All economic development must be sustainable, according to the organization's management plan. Like La Milpa, Hill Bank boards ecotourists, who want to learn more about the rain forest in its exotic setting. Guests sleep in a rustic dormitory with composting toilets, solar-powered lights, and private balconies overlooking the quiet lagoon. By day they take forest tours, spot birds, and swim in the clear, fresh waters that once carried logs to market.

Tourist income alone is not yet enough to keep Programme for Belize afloat, so the organization is presently attempting small-scale sustainable logging on 50,000 acres. Darrell Novelo, a PFB forester, took me several miles into the jungle to a tract recently harvested by a contractor. Using a Global Positioning System (GPS) that determines location by satellite, PFB mapped the tract. The GPS allows Novelo and others to divide the land into quadrants so small that a single person's location can be pinpointed anywhere on the 50,000 acres. Using that technique, they mapped every tree of commercial size.

"When we're ready to harvest, we know exactly what trees we want to take and exactly where they are," he said. "We know when they are near sensitive areas, such as streams or a bog or maybe a Maya mound, so we can take extra care or leave them standing."

We stood on a narrow logging road where the most recent cut had been made. In the distance, a troop of howler monkeys roared like jaguars in a family argument. Rain threatened, and the moist air pressed down on us like a hot blanket. Perspiration washed away our insect repellent and brought the hum of mosquitoes. A beautiful blue morpho butterfly fluttered by—one of Nazario Ku's protégés?

This was classic rain forest, and the disturbance from the timber harvest was barely noticeable—a stump here, a bent branch there, and a dim trail where a log had been snaked out after being felled. All efforts are made to be sure that the traces left behind a logging operation are minimal. A PFB staff member rides on each tractor pulling logs from the jungle, making sure that saplings are not smashed and that the butt of the log is lifted so it doesn't gouge trenches that might erode.

The small-scale operation has not yet turned a profit, said Darrell, mostly because foreign buyers are unfamiliar with some of the species being cut.

"There's a good market for mahogany and cedar, but not many of them are left," he said. "Buyers have never heard of Billy Webb wood, black cabbage bark, and the bullet tree, although they are all hardwoods with beautiful grains. And durable—the bullet tree is so hard, you can barely drive a nail into it.

"But the care we take in extracting it means the lumber is certified as being cut in an environmentally sound way. Because of public awareness of environmental issues, some companies are starting to insist on certified lumber. They just have to get familiar with some of our woods."

Enough mahogany and wildlife remain in Rio Bravo to attract poachers. Six uniformed PFB rangers bunk at Hill Bank and patrol the forest by foot, canoe, and car in search of illegal activity. Surveillance is often hampered by aging equipment. As I toured jungle roads one day with Hill Bank director Roberto Potts, our geriatric Land Rover suddenly stopped. A radioed call to Hill Bank brought another vehicle to rescue us, but in towing us back, that vehicle broke down as well.

The six rangers were grounded for several days, unable to patrol their quarter million acres. When they do, they carry no weapons. "Most illegal activity consists of an individual shooting a deer for his family or cutting logs to build a shed," Ramon had told me. A warning from the ranger usually stops it. If the situation looks more dangerous, the ranger leaves and returns with an armed policeman, which is usually sufficient. "We don't want to arm our rangers, because we think it invites a gunfight. Belize is not a violent society. There is respect for the law here."

NOT SO IN GUATEMALA, MY NEXT STOP. Although large national parks have been established here, farmers carve out new *fincas,* or farms, within park boundaries. Private loggers run mule trains of cut mahogany down jungle trails. Armed soldiers sent to expel the squatters or stop tree cutting have themselves been captured by angry citizens.

Torn for decades by conflict between insurgents and government troops, Guatemala lacks the will or the trained personnel to protect its vast forest areas. In 1990, the Maya Biosphere Reserve, capping the entire north end of the country, was designated by legislative decree. One of the reserve's core areas, the half-million-acre Sierra del Lacandon National Park was established even though guerrillas still operated there. The government also founded an agency to protect the park areas, called the Consejo Nacional de Areas Protegidas (CONAP)—National Council for Protected Areas.

When a peace treaty ended the conflict in 1996, thousands of young men had known nothing but fighting for years, and they still had their weapons. Many turned to crime—kidnapping, robbery, lynching, poaching—and a war-weary government, leery of appearing heavy-handed and sparking a new civil war, seemed powerless to stop them. Loggers cut trees almost at will, and *campesinos* (farmers) burned tracts to plant their crops—all within supposedly managed lands.

A Nature Conservancy employee working in Guatemala, John Beavers became one of the first protectors of the Lacandon reserves. The government asked him to survey Lacandon while opposing forces still operated under its dense foliage. Once hostilities ended, since few in the government had ever been trained in managing wilderness, the Conservancy enlisted a new Guatemalan environmental group, Defensores de la Naturaleza— Defenders of Nature—to help defend the northern areas. Now the Conservancy, Defensores, and the government's CONAP work together to save the rain forest and the species that live in it. A Defensores employee, Marie Claire Paiz, currently acts as director of Lacandon Park, the equivalent of someone from The Nature Conservancy running Yellowstone.

I FLEW OVER LACANDON IN A SINGLE-ENGINE PLANE with U.S.-educated Marie Claire, whose confidence and energy allow her to administer a half-million-acre park—not easy for a young woman in a macho society. We looked down on a green carpet that stretched to the horizon, interrupted by a few remote lakes that glittered like diamonds set in jade. Lighter spots of green marked wetlands where waterbirds find food and sanctuary. We saw a few dark cylindrical shapes: limestone sinkholes, as if a giant had pogoed across the land.

Within this Eden live creatures great and small, jaguars and tapirs, monkeys and coatimundis, a world of birds and a universe of insects. As we flew along the northeastern border, we also saw great square bites being taken out of this thick green carpet, evidence of grazing cattle and slash-and-burn agriculture.

"Some 35,000 people live in and around the park itself," said Marie Claire as we looked down on the illegal settlements. "We try to discourage them from spreading further by explaining to them that the law prohibits the government from building roads to them, and so they will never have electricity or medical help nearby. A few have agreed to move out, as long as we find them an alternative place to farm, with access to better infrastructure and services."

The sheer size of the forest has protected it so far. The huge green cap of the Maya Biosphere Reserve, of which Lacandon is a part, comprises nearly four million acres in the heart of the Maya forest that extends from Guatemala to Mexico and Belize and forms the largest chunk of contiguous American forest north of the Amazon. The thickest jungle, however, can disappear, one small bite at a time.

Relocating squatters has proven dangerous in Guatemala. A CONAP forest ranger told me of being with an army contingent in 1997 that drove trucks into Laguna del Tigre National Park, north of Lacandon, attempting to relocate a group of squatters who had, in principle, agreed to move. The contingent was captured by a mob of armed and angry farmers. "They disarmed us and put us in one of the trucks without food or water," the ranger told me. "They said they were going to set fire to the truck and burn us alive. One man escaped and ran 16 kilometers to report what had happened. Our release was negotiated, and the people were allowed to stay on the land."

Now, three years later, I was driven to the same rebellious community on the northeastern border of Lacandon by Marie Claire and John Beavers. We bounced for hours over a punishing road lined by simple huts. In this Guatemalan lowland, known as the Petén, farmers have been encouraged to homestead. Those on the right side of the road were legal; those on the left were in park lands. Cornfields climbed the steep hills and melded into jungle.

Naranjo, the town nearest to where the 1997 incident occurred, could have been carved out of the 19th-century American West. Crude restaurants, plank wood bars, and stores selling farm tools, saddles, and cheap clothing lined the single dusty street. Alternating with occasional pickup trucks, gaunt horses stood slack-hipped at hitching posts, and dogs and chickens browsed for scraps in the street.

The stores and bars ended at the waters of the San Pedro River and, in plain view, a long, motor-driven pirogue growled downstream, loaded with human cargo. "Illegal emigrants, heading for Mexico, and then planning to cross the border into the U.S.," John explained. Clearly law enforcement had no presence here.

We lunched on tortillas fried over an open fire at a small restaurant—two tables under a covering of thatch. The town official whose wife ran the establishment told us that the new ranger post just completed upriver was well built, that it would help protect the park. The optimistic conversations cheered my companions.

"Attitudes are getting better," said Marie Claire after we returned to the street. "I'm encouraged, for example, that the sign we saw on the road announcing the park has been there several weeks and has not been torn down."

"Conservation is a long-term process," added John. "You've got to keep your eye on the big picture."

We borrowed a speedboat to go see the new ranger post. Away from the road, the banks of the river were lined with forest and few farms. Sometimes the vista opened into broad wetlands, host to waterbirds from the U.S. during winter months. For a taste of life off the main stream, we powered up a smaller creek where trees arched out from green banks. Cormorants arrowed overhead and a small snake wigwagged through the clear water. John said that 20-pound snook could be hooked with rod and reel from such tributaries.

We reached the command post, little more than a mile from the western border with Mexico. A handsome building of white stucco, it will sit alongside a new road scheduled to be built, paralleling the river to Naranjo. Behind the post rose the highlands of Lacandon, unbroken by pasture or cornfield. Will the new road bring more settlers, more incursions into the park? Will the soldiers and their government have the will to keep them out?

We returned to the little frontier town in late afternoon and ducked under the awning of a streetside bar. *"La cerveza esta fria?*—Is the beer cold?" I smilingly asked a patron at the bar as he emptied one. *"Más o menos,"* he answered, waggling his hand, and, clutching three more bottles by their necks, he staggered off to a boat to be ferried across the river.

Bars are the refuges of frontiers, where the bored and the unlucky can drown their concerns, and drowning was well underway that late afternoon. Six months earlier on this same road, fourteen soldiers and two rangers were arresting a mahogany poacher when locals captured them, beat them with the flat sides of machetes, then released them. After my query about the beer temperature, all conversation ceased and the faces around the counter grew impassive as stone. Improved attitudes or not, it seemed a good time for a gringo and his park-protective friends to drain their beers and head out of Dodge.

WHAT WILL GUATEMALA DO with the thousands who seek a living from land that seems empty? Some find work in logging, for trees are legally and carefully extracted in multiuse areas of the Maya Biosphere Reserve and Lacandon. The nation now sells more lumber certified as coming from community-run operations than anyone in the world.

Like Belize, Guatemala also hopes that tourists drawn to the great forests will create jobs and income. Well-heeled outsiders would boat up a creek and pay top dollar for a secluded lodge amid green mansions. Tour companies would be needed to book them, and cooks, maids, boatmen, and fishing guides would see to their needs in the forest. Treks into Lacandon Park would offer a jungle experience without disturbing the forest wildlife.

To explore the southern, unsettled side of Lacandon, we drove to the town of Bethel at the edge of the park on the Usumacinta River. A clear, blue river in the dry season, with white-water rapids and sand beaches, the Usumacinta was a swollen giant in the wet. It filled the valley from one tree-lined bank to the other and whipped up wicked whirlpools. Watched by village dogs whose hipbones threatened to poke through their mangy skins, we boarded another powerboat for a trip downriver.

Pushing through with a 75-horsepower outboard motor, our boatman dodged floating logs, dead horses, and sometimes whole trees carried along in the flood. His skills were apparent in his nickname, "Perro de Agua"—otter or, literally, river dog. Overhead towered inky clouds that opened suddenly in a drenching tropical rain. Sheets of water flailed us, punctuated by flashes of lightning that moved closer until bolts and booms came almost simultaneously. Exposed on the wide river, we pulled to the bank and lingered under overhanging tree branches until the lightning passed, although light rain continued.

Lacandon Park lay on our right, Mexico's Chiapas on our left, the before and after of human settlement. To the right, trees rose one hundred feet, festooned with vines

A red-eyed tree frog shinnies up a plant that matches its eyes in a Belize rain forest.
Three inches long, the frog lays eggs on a leaf over still water, and five days later tadpoles wriggle off
for their first swim. A third of all Earth's species may live in disappearing rain forests.

above and with thick understory at their bases, living factories for turning carbon dioxide into oxygen. The green wall looked impenetrable, indestructible, but a glance to the right showed that the thickest forest can be cleared with a single match. Although some patches of jungle persisted on the Chiapas side, fires had cleared lowlands, climbed hillsides, cleaned out underbrush, and killed the big trees so that only their charred skeletons remained. Cornstalks grew where the jaguar once prowled.

After hours on the river, we stopped for the night at a site that had been a guerrilla base during the civil war but was now a station for CONAP forest guards. The CONAP guards stay for 20-day tours, sleeping under the metal roof of the one permanent building, patrolling forest trails in two- and three-day excursions. We brought them a chunk of beef to relieve the monotony of rice and beans. Four of them guard much of the ground area that took Marie Claire and me nearly three hours to fly over.

"We need eight to ten guards at this station to do the job right," said the chief ranger, Mauro Rosales, as we rolled thin slices of beef, rice, and beans in tortillas fried in their cookshed.

"The government is not providing enough money to hire that many," explained Marie Claire, "and nongovernment supporters usually don't want to pay for basic park operations. They all want to donate funds toward concrete products."

On the river trip we had met a pirogue carrying German tourists on an adventure tour, traveling from Mexico to Bethel, Guatemala. "Just upriver from us is a Maya ruin called Piedras Negras," said John. "If it were restored and those nine tourists had paid a $20 entrance fee to see it, that would total $180, enough to keep a park guard in the field for a month."

On their patrols, the guards look for animal poachers, log cutters, illegal settlers, and gatherers of the tiger palm, a small tropical plant popular as an ornamental in the southern United States. Like the sabal palm gathered for thatch, the tiger palm can survive removal of a leaf or two for commerce, but greedy harvesters often take the whole plant, threatening its existence. John says plantations of tiger palm are being considered as an alternative to wild gathering. The guards encounter many of the forest's natural dwellers— monkeys, tapirs, coatimundis, peccaries, deer, and numerous birds. They see tracks of jaguar and puma but rarely the secretive cats themselves.

In an hour's walk to Piedras Negras the next morning, I also tasted Lacandon's mystery. A nightjar fluttered up in the dim light under the forest canopy, then quickly settled again out of concern for a nearby nest. A troop of spider monkeys crossed over us high above, aerialists leaping from branch to branch. Leafcutter ants crossed the path in miniature single-file convoys, holding aloft their triangular cargoes like green sails. Fat white grubs as big as my thumb sprawled on the forest floor, recyclers of rotting vegetation who turn it into fertile soil, pumping nutrients back into the trees. The rich scent of damp foliage and fallen leaves filled our nostrils. Without warning, we stood in the remnants of a once great city.

Restored Maya sites give one a sense of the communities that once existed, but unrestored sites like Piedras Negras have their own poignant charms. The awe of past grandeur mingles with the sobering realization of the tenuous nature of success upon viewing crumbling temples and grand stairways laced with thick vines. One might as well be walking through downtown Denver a millennium hence, with conifers growing through pavement cracks, sagebrush covering sidewalks, and vultures launching from roosts in the U.S. Mint.

The stairway mounting the main temple must have rivaled the entrance to the U.S. Capitol, but now it is covered with forest debris. We climbed to the sacrificial altar at the top, which in the Maya heyday would have been a grand final view of the city below for war captives before priests splashed their blood on the stones. We strolled through the bedrooms of courtiers and princesses. We stooped to enter sweat baths where royalty relaxed on benches while slaves poured water over hot rocks to make steam.

Then back to the boat for the long return trip upriver to Bethel, this time battling against the current. As we pulled into a side creek for a quiet lunch, a large crocodile, perhaps seeking the same, splashed and disappeared. Compared to the brown, swollen Usumacinta, silt-laden from agricultural runoff, this jungle-filtered stream remained clear, and we looked down on the tops of submerged bushes.

CLARITY ABOUT RAIN FOREST VIRTUES seems to be filtering down to the people of Guatemala. "They are getting more comfortable with the idea of conservation," said John. "At first there was much talk of 'Why are you taking this away from us? Why can't we cut as many trees as we want?' Now people see that managed timber can create income, and that tourists pay real money to explore ruins and forest."

"Even the workers in CONAP didn't understand fully what they were doing at first," added Marie Claire. "They just did what they were told and took no pride in it. Now several of them show good initiative in doing the job."

I remembered the eloquence of chief ranger Mauro Rosales over breakfast at the ranger station that morning. A former timber gatherer and tiger palm collector himself, he has seen both sides of Guatemalans' struggle to understand the green wealth that surrounds them. He was among those army troops terrorized by villagers who didn't want to be relocated. As a forest guard, he once stood beside the head of a managed timber operation when the man was shot and killed by opponents to forest regulations. The killers were later arrested and given prison sentences.

"Since I began working for CONAP, I have learned the importance of preserving the forest, not only for myself but for my sons and grandsons," said Mauro. "Just by walking in the forest you can see its value—the possibility of people paying to see it, the opportunity to study it, and the beauty of the many creatures that live here." A man with a sixth-grade education, he spoke with the wisdom of a sage. If the message reaches enough of his countrymen, the green belt of Mesoamerica may yet be saved. ■

central &
south america
portfolio

～

SPLENDID DESOLATION *meets the bountiful depths*
at an island in Mexico's Sea of Cortés, *where unique*
land creatures live near a treasury of marine life.
In parts of Central and South America
once deemed too vast and isolated
to be threatened by human incursions,
species now require urgent protection
to survive.

CLOUDS BLANKET volcanic cones and
desert lands at El Pinacaté Biosphere
Preserve, one of the driest places on the
North American continent, just south of
Yuma, Arizona. U.S. astronauts once prac-
ticed for a moon landing on these extinct
volcanoes: undisturbed by erosion, geology frozen in time. Despite the barren
appearance, plants, animals, and people
stake claims to the dry terrain, part of the
vast 55-million-acre Sonoran ecoregion
that sprawls over northern Mexico,
Arizona, and California. Endangered
pronghorn gallop across the border into
U.S. properties that include the Cabeza
Prieta National Wildlife Refuge and a
defense department training range. Hundreds of bird species migrate through,
breed, or reside here permanently. Sonoran
riches include some 300 types of cactuses.

To counter human pressures threatening
to change the area, The Nature Conservancy
joined a binational team to identify conservation sites. Protection could ensure
survival of the ecoregion's biodiversity.

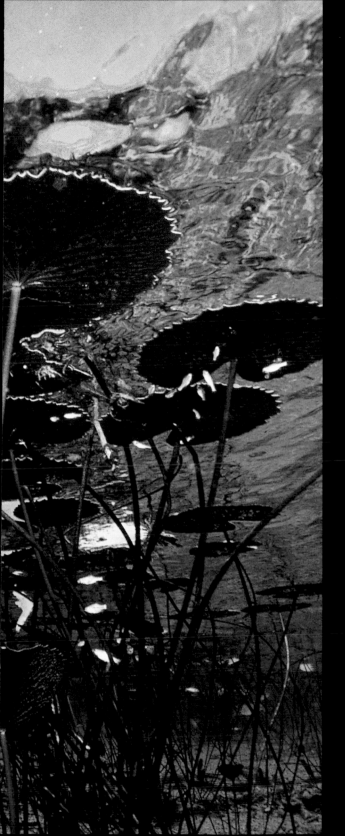

RAFTS OF WATER lilies shade pupfish,
tetras, and cichlids at Cuatro Ciénagas
(Four Marshes) in the Chihuahuan desert.
Amid extreme temperature variation and
high mineral content, the crystal-clear
waters and surrounding desert harbor
more than 80 species that live only here,
including cactuses, snails, scorpions, fish,
and reptiles. One species of fish can survive
in a hot saline environment when stranded
in small pools. Box turtles, normally land-
lubbers, take to the water. Gabbling on the
surface are Mexican ducks and migratory
waterfowl. Some pools are mere aquariums
while others measure 250 feet wide.

Agriculture has siphoned off badly
needed moisture, lowering some pools
three to four feet and drying up others.
Concern for the oasis led the Mexican government to protect part of Cuatro Ciénagas as a national biological refuge in 1994.
In 2000, The Nature Conservancy and a
local partner, Pronatura Noreste, bought
another 7,000 acres of critical habitat.

SHEDDING A WATERFALL off 12-foot flukes, a blue whale begins a dive between Baja California and the mainland of Mexico. Only 30 miles wide, the wedge known in Mexico as the Sea of Cortés and in the U.S. as the Gulf of California plunges sometimes a mile deep. Upwellings of cold, nutrient-rich water draw more than 800 species of fish and 2,000 species of invertebrates, plus predators such as marlin, snapper, yellowfin tuna—and whales, such as the giant blue.

The superproductive fishery also attracts pirate fleets of fishermen, who use illegal methods such as night fishing with lights, gill nets, and drift nets, which kill indiscriminately. Coastal development on land also threatens land species endemic to the Baja. To stop the carnage, The Nature Conservancy works with local conservation organizations, the Mexican Navy, and Mexican environ-mental agencies in policing the sea and creating sound ecoregional plans.

BOLE-DEEP DURING flood stage, palm trees frame waterfalls of Canaima, at 7.4 million acres one of the largest national parks in the world. Wind and water in the Guiana Highlands have carved cliffs in the sandstone, forming islands of vegetation called *tepuis* that thrust into the air like giant corks. Their sheer-sided isolation inspired Sir Arthur Conan Doyle's *Lost World,* a fictional account of marooned dinosaurs. Off one of these tepuis, three-quarters of a mile high, plummets Angel Falls, Earth's highest waterfall.

If not dinosaurs, rare plants and a primitive people have found refuge in Canaima's jungles and heights. On one plateau live 96 bird species, 29 of them found nowhere else. Many plants have yet to be identified. Jungle dwellers known as the Pemon people deplete resources as their numbers increase. The Nature Conservancy and local partners help the Venezuelan government devise better park management and train the Pemon as guides and forest protectors.

HIGHLAND WATER collectors, treelike fraillejones *(Espletia hartwegiana)* spread velvety leaves that gather dew from clouds rolling through the Andes at elevations of around 10,000 feet. The plants transfer their excess moisture to the soil, therefore becoming the principal source of groundwater in the high, cloudy, but nearly rainless plateaus known as *paramos.* Although fraillejones remain common in the upper reaches of Colombia and Venezuela, the El Angel Nature Reserve in Ecuador represents their southernmost extension. Provincial Ecuadorian officials set aside the reserve to protect its water-holding capacity and numerous species, but they failed to compensate landowners. In protest, farmers continue potato production, threatening the natural hydrologic process. New management plans—minimal agriculture, income from tourism, and selling water resources downstream—could provide locals with a livelihood while protecting a unique ecosystem.

FLASHBACK TO THE primeval, a marine iguana clambers over cooled lava as fresh flows light the nighttime sky over the Galápagos Islands. Other unique island residents include 600-pound tortoises, the rare waved albatross, and 13 species of finch descended from a common ancestor. The islands became an evolutionary touchstone after 19th-century naturalist Charles Darwin wrote of long isolated species adapting to unique Galápagos circumstances in *On the Origin of Species.* Despite protections, both vegetation and wildlife in the Galápagos suffer depredation from cats, dogs, pigs, goats, rats, and a swelling human population. The Nature Conservancy participates in a study of policies to reduce the human impact.

GALÁPAGOS TORTOISES cool in a seasonal puddle. Predation by humans and introduced species has reduced their numbers to fewer than 20,000.

A PAIR of waved albatrosses bill and coo, part of an elaborate bonding ritual

GRANITE MOUNTAINS stand like sentinels above an expanse of the Atlantic Forest, which once stretched uninterrupted along Brazil's east coast. Less than 7 percent remains, shrunk by logging, grazing, and residential development. Largest of the intact sections, the 774,000-acre Guaraqueçaba in the Atlantic Forest Environmental Protection Area offers a glimpse of biological wealth at risk. Here live rare golden lion tamarins—fewer than a thousand remain in the wild; rainbows of orchids; and the largest New World simian, the wooly spider monkey. Elevations vary from coastal levels to 5,000 feet, creating numerous ecozones and hosting millions of species.

Most of this area is privately owned land, sprinkled with small communities. The Nature Conservancy now works with Brazilian conservation groups to protect further the land and restore the forests. In a deal brokered by the Conservancy, Brazilians plant trees on 41,500 acres purchased by two U.S. corporations.

THE EASTERN UNITED

STATES

Fog lends mystery to 15-acre Lehigh Pond in the
Pocono Mountains of Pennsylvania, a glacial
kettle amid 40,000 acres of protected state land.

Fall paints blueberries and maples at Bruce Lake in a Pennsylvania natural area.

wilderness
within reach

At first light we nosed a canoe into
Tunkhannock Creek and rode it downstream.
The world hung in such hush that water dripping
from our paddles seemed to echo off
the conifers a hundred yards away.
In the open, shrub-filled valley the green
banks pressed close, and beneath us
aquatic grasses billowed in the current
like a woman's long hair.

As we meandered through lazy loops a deer, startled by our silent approach, leaped desperately for the opposite shore and landed at mid-creek with a deafening splash. After a few frenzied strokes, it emerged on the other side to plunge into rhododendron without pausing to shake dry. A great blue heron, skimming at brush-top level, whooshed nearly into our hats, rearing in surprise to gain altitude.

A sense of the primeval hung over Tunkhannock Creek. We could have been native Minisink hunters seeking game in 1580, or farmers led by William Penn a century later, looking for fertile soils. Instead we were moderns in a world of cell phones and computers, relishing wildlands a two-hour car ride from Philadelphia or New York City. The brushy flats in Pennsylvania through which we floated were owned by the city of Bethlehem some 60 miles downstream, which keeps the watershed natural to provide fresh, clean water to its residents.

One gem among a high crown of jewels, Tunkhannock Creek lies at the southern edge of a plateau known as the Poconos. A tableland with steep ridges cut by streams, not a mountain system, the Poconos stand above surrounding terrain at an elevation that nurtures plant and animal communities not found at lower levels. The mosaic of lakes, bogs, peatlands, forests, heath, and oak barrens annually draws thousands of urbanites from the world of streetlights to one of sylvan calm.

Paddling in the stern of my canoe was Ellen Lott of the northeast Pennsylvania office of The Nature Conservancy, which wants to keep portions of the Poconos forever wild. The lands owned by Bethlehem remain unchanged for now. Elsewhere, through outright purchases of property, sometimes in partnership with other organizations, the Conservancy has protected some 13,000 acres in the region. A thousand more have been saved by arranging conservation easements with property owners. Preserved along with wildland peace are a number of unique natural communities.

The Tunkhannock watershed, for example, is the only ecosystem of its kind in the world. The 32 square miles of swamps, forests, oak barrens, and a few farm fields hold one of the world's highest concentration of rare plants and animals. Beleaguered but enduring species include whip-poor-wills, bobolinks, northern harriers, river otters, and more than 30 species of rare butterflies, moths, and damselflies. Beavers and some of the world's largest black bears thrive here, as do snowshoe hares, normally found much farther north.

The Tunkhannock flows only 17 miles before emptying into Tobyhanna Creek, a tributary of the Lehigh River. For part of that journey it widens into shallow open water called Long Pond, lined with marshes and framed by forests of red maple, spruce, and tamarack. The National Audubon Society has called Long Pond and its environs one of the most important bird areas in Pennsylvania, and The Nature Conservancy has included it on a list of Earth's last great places. Pulling over to an open stretch of shoreline hours later to end our voyage, we hauled out amid a crowd of bird-watchers.

Forces of geology and climate teamed up to shape the biological oasis known as the Poconos. As Earth's crustal plates shifted 280 million years ago, the pressure caused some of that rock to fold like a carpet, forming high ridges—the Appalachian Mountains. The Poconos, made of sterner stuff, rose like an elevator, lifting a nearly level mass a thousand feet above its surroundings.

Eons later, glaciers bore down from the north, scouring depressions and leaving piles of debris that dammed up water into lakes. The result is a 300-square-mile corner of northeastern Pennsylvania that resembles northern peatlands, as if a piece of Canada had drifted down to lie marooned between New York and New Jersey.

The entire plateau remained an island of wilderness long after its surroundings knew human settlement. The Native Americans known as the Minisink followed game to the cooler heights in summer, but their permanent lodges were in the more fertile Delaware River Valley—hence the name "Delaware," given them by white settlers. When Charles II granted Quaker William Penn a colony that became dedicated to religious tolerance, most of the new "Pennsylvanians" settled in the southeast, around Philadelphia.

As more Europeans poured into Pennsylvania and Indian influence waned, hunting trails through the Poconos became horse-and-wagon roads. By the mid-1700s, a growing northeastern population brought to the plateau loggers who floated cut trees down the Delaware and Lehigh Rivers. Entrepreneurs noted the swift-flowing streams pouring off the plateau and built mills for grinding grain, sawing logs, and weaving wool from sheep raised on the bared hills. A trickle of 19th-century tourists came from Philadelphia in horse-drawn carriages to escape the summer heat.

With the gradual reforesting of the plateau and the coming of railroads, the trickle became a flood. A thousand miles of clear streams and 30,000 acres of lakes drew fishermen, hunters, artists, and nature lovers. George Innes painted two oils showing the Delaware Water Gap. Actress Sarah Bernhardt could be seen strolling the sidewalks of fashionable resort towns. Western writer Zane Grey wrote most of his novels here from 1905 to 1918. With many romantic waterfalls spilling over sandstone ledges, the Poconos became popular with honeymooners. Summer vacationers seeking active recreation spawned golf courses, tennis courts, riding and hiking trails, and ski lodges.

The Poconos long remained a tourist destination with few permanent residents. Beyond the golf greens and the sound of pool splashes lay tangled woods and quiet streams. In the 1970s, construction of superhighways made the cool, wooded plateau a bedroom community for long-distance commuters to the big cities. Housing developments sprang up, and fast-food eateries and convenience stores followed. Tunkhannock Township, which includes Long Pond, had a population of 224 in 1860 and only 317 in 1970. With the completion of Interstate 80, the number leapt to 2,144 within ten years. Today some areas of the Poconos are growing at 300 times the rate of the rest of Pennsylvania.

A bald eagle wintering on the Delaware River soars over the Poconos in search of a meal. Numerous eagles nest along the river.

Rhododendron and gray birch grow in the Poconos, where glaciers gouged depressions, piled up debris, and left in their wake a

terrain that fosters heath, forest, swamp, peat bog, and barrens.

"I didn't see this development coming," said Francis Altemose, who has lived near Long Pond since 1936. Once a farmer of garden vegetables for market, he now produces hay and oats for new residents' pleasure horses. "I ran bulldozers to help build Interstate 80, and I just thought it would be a convenient way for people to get to New York City, not a way for them to live here and work there. The new roads have been the ruination of this area. At least we still have public lands and land saved by the Conservancy."

One of the latter is the 2,200-acre Thomas Darling Preserve, named for a gentle naturalist and bought by The Nature Conservancy, the Wildlands Conservancy, and Tobyhanna Township to save critical wildlife habitat. Three hundred more acres connected to it are in conservation easement. The woods provide a tenement for the avian world, with top floors in the branches of red spruce, American larch, hemlock, red maple, and balsam fir; mid-levels among young trees and tall shrubs; and a ground floor of blueberry bushes, sheep laurel, and black huckleberry.

I JOINED A GROUP OF VISITING Ecuadorian conservationists who came to see birds they also see in their native country. Both the Conservancy and the Ecuadorians participate in the Migratory Bird Program, funded by Canon USA, Inc., and aimed at improving the chances of survival for migratory birds. Habitats are disappearing in both countries, as are stopover forests where the birds rest and feed during their journeys. Largely as a result of migratory complications, more than 25 percent of bird species in the Americas are considered at risk. Conservationists in both countries have exchanged visits to see how each deals with the problem.

Leading our early morning walk was Doug Gross, a local ornithologist, who wore a baseball cap turned backward and a look of secret mirth. As we moved slowly through the woods, an ovenbird with a nest nearby perched on a low branch and scolded us nervously.

"Its nest is on the ground, with a cover over the top and one entrance on the side, like an old-fashioned bread oven," Doug explained. "The cover hides the eggs and young from bird predators and squirrels that might see them from above. Ovenbirds are in trouble now because an excessive deer population overbrowses the low shrubs that help hide the nest and that also shelter the insects that the birds feed upon."

The first shared bird we saw was a veery, a kind of thrush that migrates to Central and South America. Another migrant, a broad-winged hawk, soared overhead, looking for chipmunks, snakes, smaller birds, frogs, and mice. The most common raptor in the Poconos, this hawk works its way in fall down the Appalachian ridge, along the coast of Texas, down the Mexican coast and into Central America, then down the Andes to winter on the east side of that range.

A scarlet tanager appeared high in a tree. It was a bird the Ecuadorians knew from their homeland, but this one sported a dazzlingly colorful summer coat unfamiliar to

Autumn's flaming signature, a sugar maple leaf rests on frosted grass in Pennsylvania's Delaware State Forest. Fall comes early to the Poconos, a tableland raised a thousand feet higher than its surroundings.

them. While wintering in their country, the male tanager's plumage stays a dreary olive green. But to attract mates in the northern spring, its color changes to brilliant red, dashed with black wings.

THE THOMAS DARLING PRESERVE'S mossy ground was spongy from two days of rain. Several miles away, near Tannersville, we visited a real swamp at the Tannersville Bog, where the earth is so insubstantial that a wooden walkway built over it floats on metal drums.

"When I was growing up near here, our mothers used to tell us, 'Don't go down to that swamp—it's dangerous,'" said Jerry Keltz, a retired electrical engineer who guided us over the walkway. "Now I give slide shows on what a fascinating place it is."

Tannersville Bog was at first a lake left by the last glaciers, he said. These bogs were formed when huge blocks of ice, left behind by retreating glaciers, melted to form what geologists call kettle-hole lakes. In a swamp-making process that took thousands of years, vegetation, primarily sphagnum moss, arched out from the shore year after year. Open water slowly shrank until it disappeared.

Eventually small shrubs, members of the heath family—leatherleaf, sheep laurel, bog laurel, bog rosemary, and blueberry—took root in the moss. The plant material died, its decay stalled by lack of oxygen, and it compacted into peat. Around the bog, trees such as black spruce and American larch grew slowly. The Nature Conservancy bought the 150-acre bog to preserve not only bird habitat but also the unique life-forms found there.

With the Ecuadorians in tow, Jerry pointed out plants that survive in soils so acidic that they hold few nutrients. The sundew's halo of sticky tentacles lie open, waiting for an insect to alight. When one lands on the open leaf, the tentacles close in and trap the insect, supplying the plant with food.

"The pitcher plant catches insects in a pool of water," Jerry explained, pointing to another carnivorous plant, this one with vaselike leaves. Flies, bugs, and moths either fly or crawl into the pitcher and then slip down the steep sides into trapped rainwater. Unable to climb back out, these creatures feed the plant with the soup of decay.

More common wildlife such as bears, coyotes, bobcats, and snowshoe hares find a home in the tangle. Dragonflies sputtered around us like World War I aircraft, and birds chorused somewhere in the thick growth. Several rare species use the preserve, including the bog copper, a butterfly that lays its eggs only on wild cranberry plants.

To the foreign visitors, Jerry Keltz himself was a rarity. "Imagine, a retired person donating his time to tell us about this special place," exclaimed a burly Ecuadorian named Bolivar. "In our country, only a few young people interested in conservation would do that."

They had yet to meet the patriarch of Poconos conservation. Ninety-year-old Dixon Miller joined the Pennsylvania State Forest Service in 1925 and has served for the past half century as a fire warden. For six weeks in spring and sometimes during summer droughts, Dixon daily climbs the 108 steps of a fire tower atop the highest point in the Poconos to watch for telltale columns of smoke.

"I've always liked elevation," he told me, admitting that part of liking elevation is that he also likes snow. "A few years ago we had a snowfall of 21 inches on the Poconos, and down below it was all rain. We get about 80 inches of snow a year."

At local ski resorts, Dixon is always the oldest on the slopes, and often the only one doing "ballet skiing." Tall and lean, if a little bent, he attributes his active life to a regimen of working out on a Stairmaster and a rowing machine in his little cabin beside the fire tower. Admirers suspect the perpetual smile on his face contributes to longevity.

Dixon Miller's summer passion is creating trails, and he has blazed 26 miles of them through Poconos state forestlands. A puckish trail maker, his routes have hikers hopscotching over pedestals of rock, climbing garage-size boulders, and descending into cool, moss-covered crevasses opened up by frost. Inner-city youngsters brought to the Poconos through the Conservancy's Urban Youth Partnership love the obstacle courses. In the meantime, they learn about career possibilities in conservation.

OUTDOOR EDUCATION APPEALS to an older generation as well. In Promised Land State Park, 3,000 acres in the northeastern Pennsylvania Poconos, I joined a group of gray-haired hikers following a Pied Piper named John Serrao, who spun an appealing tale of forest lore.

"This is wood sorrel, which has leaves like a clover," he said, bending to trailside. "It's one of the few wild plants to bloom in mid-summer.

"Hear that bird? It's a red-eyed vireo. You're not hearing many birds this time of year because singing is a way of attracting mates, and by now most have found one and settled down to raise a family."

He pointed to a bulbous growth on an oak sapling and explained: "A wasp lays an egg on the sapling and injects an enzyme into the plant that makes the stem grow into a cottony ball around the egg. When the larva hatches, it feeds on the plant tissue, sheltered from predators by the cottony ball around it. As an adult, it struggles to the surface and flies away."

"This is my 15th walk this year," said blue-jeaned Karen Livingood, a psychologist who now wore a necklace of binoculars. "There are things in my life that are so wearing, and being out here and learning things through John just lifts me."

For all his cheerful demeanor, their trim, athletic leader is no dreamy-eyed idealist. "I moved here because it's a place that still has otters and bears," John told me, "but I'm not optimistic that the Poconos is going to keep its wildlife. The amount of development is very depressing, including talk of building an industrial park."

Perhaps a million skiers flock to the slopes of seven resorts from December through March, bringing at least 200 million dollars in income and spawning more

A bobcat prowls in winter on 2,200-acre Thomas Darling Preserve, one of Pennsylvania's largest undisturbed peatlands. Wildlife large and small thrives in wild pockets within commuting distance of New York and Philadelphia.

condominiums. Blue Ridge Real Estate Company owns two of the resorts and is also the biggest property owner in the Poconos, with holdings of some 30,000 acres. A third of that property has been turned into ski resorts and housing developments, and a plan has been drawn for developing another 10,000 acres. The last block of 10,000 acres is being left open for now. "I grew up here, and I'm not going to mess up this beautiful area," said the company's president, Gary Smith.

A 1992 Harvard study of development in Monroe County, the heart of the Poconos, painted a bleak picture for preservationists. The study concluded that if growth continued under the current zoning requirements, by 2020 the county, now with 130,000 people, will have grown to 600,000 and will, essentially, be a suburb. Alarmed by the prediction, residents formed Monroe 2020 to envision a more appealing future. The developers, conservationists, engineers, and landowners drew up a plan that includes considerable open space with houses clustered in areas less sensitive to development.

The plan anticipates that Monroe County's population might be held to only 300,000 in the next 20 years. "To protect what we all came up here to enjoy, to protect water and open space, we've got to control building sprawl," said Wes Shirk, who has been visiting the Poconos for half a century and has lived there full-time since 1983. "It's just a matter of working out the legalities."

Private groups have already taken steps. Wes and his wife, Jeanne, live in Pocono Lake Preserve, a private community of 5,000 acres restricted to 140 members. Each member personally owns only two or three acres and the remainder, commonly owned, stays open for hiking trails and wildlife habitat. Residents are required to build back from the shore, to remove signs of human presence, and to drain their septic systems well away from the lake.

"We have a rich supply of unpolluted water in the Poconos," said Wes, "but to keep it that way, we have to protect the watershed."

As we talked in the community office and post office overlooking Pocono Lake, a large bird swooped over the mirror-flat water before us. "Look, an osprey," he said, pointing. "They were plentiful here in the 1960s, but they nearly disappeared when DDT made their eggshells fragile. Then chicks transferred here from the Chesapeake Bay area reproduced well, and now there are hundreds again."

Interest in retaining the wild flavor in the Poconos appears to be gaining steam. In 1999, voters passed a referendum authorizing Monroe County to borrow 25 million dollars to retain clean water and open space. Watershed associations have been formed to educate people about the value of saving the natural forest in order to ensure a water supply.

NATURAL FORESTS DESERVE SAVING for pure pleasure, too. With science teacher and naturalist Patti O'Keefe, I ventured onto 750 acres purchased by The Nature Conservancy and turned over to Pennsylvania for use as state game lands. Our destination was one of the glacial depressions known as Lost Lakes, because of their isolation in verdant timber growth. The first part of the walk was on a wide path, mowed clean for several yards on either side—an effortless stroll except for occasional barriers of carefully placed logs.

Someone out there hates ATVs—all-terrain vehicles, the growling little four-wheel-drives that give hunters a wider range but change the forest ambience. To deter them, interlocking fences of logs and brush have been secretly constructed from one line of trees to the other across the trail every several hundred yards. Neither the state game commission nor The Nature Conservancy supports the use of ATVs, but both parties deny responsibility for the barriers. So they remain, a vigilante effort to preserve forest quiet.

Patti brings groups of youngsters and adults on the path in a Nature Conservancy summer program, revealing a wealth of little-known secrets of the Eastern woods. She points out club moss, used by Indian shamans to dazzle their followers because when dried and tossed on a fire, it flares up impressively. At a beaver pond she uses a stick to fish a strand of bladderwort up from underwater. Tiny aquatic animals swimming near the water plant trigger small sacs that inflate suddenly, then suck in the creatures and digest their nutrients.

The biggest secret is the way to the Lost Lakes. Patti led me off the main trail onto a side path that eventually dead-ended in a small clearing amid a thick patch of rhododendron. "Now for the secret passage," she said slyly, and like a butler swiveling a bookcase to show access into a secret room, she pulled aside a portion of shrubs. Ahead lay a faint route through the crooked rhododendron branches. After a gymnastic few minutes of stepping high, leaning over, and bending back through the maze, we emerged again into open woods and a short time later arrived on the deserted shores of a small lagoon.

I would like to say we then assembled portable fishing rods and hauled out finny behemoths—but the locked-in waters are naturally acidic, too acidic for fish. A line of tall trees and green shrubs around a little visited and unspoiled lake provided satisfaction enough, though. Jays cried in the treetops. A woodpecker drummed on a dead snag. Asphalt and traffic could have been a thousand miles away.

After long minutes of admiring the scene, we retraced our steps, contorted our way back through the rhodo maze, clambered over the many barriers on the main trail, and returned to our car.

I couldn't have made it without my guide. "Getting lost" is a relative term in 750 acres of timber—but you could end up miles from your car and be very late for supper. It was comforting to know that in the Eastern woods one can still find isolation, deep quiet, and an air of mystery, thanks to set-aside lands, a phantom barrier builder, and a secret passage. ∎

Frost rimes bushes and boulders in the Moosic Mountains at the western edge of the Poconos. High, rugged terrain that delayed settlement now attracts urban residents, spurring efforts to protect remaining wildlands.

eastern
united states
portfolio

∾

CYPRESS SWAMPS FRINGE the Altamaha River as it
winds through the coastal plains of Georgia.
In the heavily populated eastern United States,
a surprising number of wild corners remain.
Often miles and minutes from urban centers,
they offer primeval quiet and harbor species
that are running out of places to hide.

FLAMELIKE TENDRILS surrounded by white fluff gave *Geum triflorum* its common name of prairie smoke. The blossom, normally found on prairies, grows in the Great Lakes region in a habitat known as alvar grasslands: thin soils lying atop limestone bedrock once scraped clean by glaciers. The strange union of Arctic tundra and Great Plains is found only in the Great Lakes and Europe's Baltic Sea basin. The combination nurtures unique plant and animal species, some existing nowhere else. Drawn to the vegetative mix are such rare and threatened birds as the upland sandpiper, osprey, tawny crescentspot, and northern harrier.

Drawn as well to these open spaces are off-road vehicles, mountain bikes, and developers building second homes. To protect the unusual ecology, The Nature Conservancy has created Maxton Plains Preserve—more than a thousand acres protected through land purchases and conservation easements—on Drummond Island in Lake Huron.

A SEEMINGLY ENDLESS carpet of wildflowers spread before the first white settlers as they entered the lands of today's Illinois. Open prairie stretched to the horizon in dueling hues, as seen in this remnant stand of goldenrod and blazing star near Chicago. A treaty promised Native Americans use of lands west of a line through the site, a promise later broken. Today 99.9 percent of Illinois's prairie has disappeared under urban development and farmland, not including this Nature Conservancy preserve known as Indian Boundary Prairies. A hundred more acres of high quality prairie lie unprotected.

The preserve harbors unusual species and some endangered ones, such as the prairie white-fringed orchid. Hordes of butterflies, including the regal fritillary, bunchgrass skipper, and dreamy dusky wing, still sip nectar here, and the declining bobolink finds sanctuary. Gray foxes and 13 amphibians and reptiles coexist in this ark for species that once thrived in an ocean of prairie.

SNOW POWDERING the banks of the
Neversink will become part of the runoff
in one of the Northeast's most pristine
rivers. A main headwater for the Delaware,
the Neversink became a candidate for
preservation because of its healthy population of imperiled dwarf wedge mussels.
Further study revealed an incredibly
diverse and intact ecosystem and the
purest source of drinking water for New
York City. In its floodplain forests, marshes,
and meadows can be found 132 species of
birds, including ospreys and bald eagles; 17
reptile species; and 14 amphibians.

Beginning with a 370-acre preserve
to protect the mussels, The Nature
Conservancy expanded the project into
a much broader freshwater initiative.
Strategies in ecologically sustainable water
management, community involvement,
and scientific study formulated along
the Neversink and other key sites could
become models for protecting freshwater
systems around the world.

A TIMELY FEAST awaits shorebirds (far right) migrating in spring from South America to the Arctic Circle. Their stop along the shores of Delaware Bay coincides with the mating of horseshoe crabs (right), whose egg masses provide fuel for millions of flyers. Despite the opportune juncture of feathers and food, the environmental diagnosis of the giant bay that touches both Delaware and New Jersey causes concern. Residential and commercial activities and the clearing of vegetative cover for agriculture have altered the shoreline and the water entering the bay. Many plant species are rare, extinct, or missing. In Delaware, 130 animal species live precarious lives.

To counter these effects, Conservancy offices in both states cooperate to conserve the rich biodiversity around the bay. Preserves are maintained on both shores to allow birds to feed and fledge chicks, and educational programs alert human visitors of the need to respect the privacy of the original residents.

PROTECTED LANDS often become islands of habitat for the species that live there, causing inbreeding among animals and isolating plants in vulnerable clumps. The Jocassee Gorges of North and South Carolina, carved by five rivers pouring off the highland plateau of the Blue Ridge, long have been the centerpiece of natural areas. Privately owned, development of the area could have exploited the gorges' scenic wonderland.

In the late 1990s, though, the two states and several conservation organizations, including the Conservation Fund and The Nature Conservancy, cooperated to buy the roughly 40,000-acre area, connecting important contiguous natural habitats into one 200,000-acre protected region.

Here, amid one of the greatest concentrations of waterfalls in the eastern United States, live black bears, bobcats, wild turkeys, several types of rare fishes, and the highest number of salamander species found in one location in the world. High rainfall levels—second highest in the continental United States—support some 60 species of rare plants as well, including 90 percent of the world's oconee bells, a plant whose nearest relatives are found in China and Japan.

FLOWERING DOGWOODS and Spanish moss streaming off live oaks offer a blizzard of beauty in the ACE Basin, one of the largest undeveloped wetlands and uplands on the Atlantic coast. Named for three rivers that flow through it—the Ashepoo, Combahee, and Edisto—the 350,000-acre coastal area includes forested uplands, a peat bog, forested wetlands, tidal marshes, and barrier islands. It supports 33 types of plant communities and several endangered species. Wood storks stalk the shallows, short-nosed sturgeons swim the waters, and loggerhead turtles nest on the beaches. Migratory waterfowl fuel up in the marshes and colorful wood ducks nest in the watery forests. Protected lands total nearly half the basin. A task force representing state and federal agencies and environmental organizations monitors the ACE's wildness.

YELLOW GOATFISH linger under a sheltering elkhorn coral in the National Marine Sanctuary in Key Largo. A crossroads between tropic and temperate zones, this string of islands arcing off the tip of Florida is a hotbed of imperiled plants and animals, such as the semaphore cactus and the tiny key deer. The six terrestrial communities include the unusual pine rocklands. Seven underwater communities are rare or imperiled, including coral reefs and sea grass beds.

The beauty of the Keys draws two and a half million visitors a year. Development has destroyed much of the pine rocklands and hardwood forests. Runoff has degraded water quality and damaged the third largest coral reef in the world. In one of its most daunting conservation challenges, The Nature Conservancy maintains two preserves—a total of more than 6,000 acres—and partners with public and private organizations in promoting environmentally sensible human activities.

STATES

The Great Sand Dunes, second highest in the world, rise above Colorado's San Luis Valley grasslands.

Wild sunflowers and snakeweed butter grasslands of the Medano-Zapata Ranch, a Nature Conservancy preserve.

where the
buffalo roam

∽

From high on the mountainside,
the hunters and their families sighted the bison
cows and calves grazing on the valley floor below.
The men descended first,
making no attempt to conceal themselves for
hours, since the animals were miles away
and merely black dots on the grassy plain.

NEAR THEIR DANGEROUS PREY the hunters crouched behind 12-foot sand dunes, selecting the cow that the others seemed to follow. Fanning out, they crept closer in the tall grass and sagebrush until they could hear grunting and the tearing of grass with teeth. Then the arm of the best hunter snapped forward and, with the spear-thrower gripped in his hand, he sent a stone-tipped projectile into the heart of the lead cow. Their leader down, the animals milled in confusion as more spears flew and animals bellowed in pain. Calves standing by their fallen mothers were killed after the rest of the herd had lumbered away.

On the ground lay 48 bison, a wealth of meat and hides. With sharp, stone knives the jubilant hunters cut into some of them, satisfying their immediate hunger with raw livers and tongues. When the others rejoined them, each family set up a camp nearby for two weeks of feasting, drying meat in the cool autumn air, and working hides into warm clothing.

The successful hunt by Paleo Indians called the Folsom people occurred some 10,000 years ago in the San Luis Valley of south-central Colorado. Two mountain ranges frame the broad plain, the Sangre de Cristo Mountains to the east and the San Juan Mountains to the west. They meet at the north end to form an irregular horseshoe around a valley 65 miles wide and 100 miles long. The open side of the horseshoe ends just south of the Colorado–New Mexico border at Ute Peak and San Antonio Mountain, convenient gateposts to Colorado's largest intermountain basin.

By careful sleuthing in the sandy soil, anthropologist Pegi Jodry re-created the hunt for me. "We know the kill sites because the front leg bones are still there," she said. "They had too little meat on them to bother carrying them to the camps, where the women flayed meat in strips for drying. Also, at campsites you find small stone chips where they resharpened spear points and replaced broken ones. There were sand dunes then, too—perhaps not in the same places—for them to hide behind, and the grasses and brush would have been taller for them to sneak close, because that was a wetter period."

Thousands of years after the hunt, in 1898, a white settler shot the valley's last wild bison. European immigrants to America had called them buffalo, the name given to wild ox of the Old World. Cattle took their place on the sandy east side of the San Luis Valley, while farmers began harvesting potatoes, wheat, and hay on the more fertile west side. Like the bison, many creatures that had lived in the valley for thousands of years were being edged out. In 1985 the owner of a ranch called the Medano returned bison to the valley to raise them for the novelty meat market. A few years later the ranch changed hands, but the bison stayed. In 1999 The Nature Conservancy bought the Medano and a neighboring spread called the Zapata, two ranches with 100,000 acres in grazing rights. The commercial bison herd came with the deal, and the land in the northeastern corner also harbored numerous bird and mammal species, including large herds of elk. The Conservancy is transforming the properties into a research and education center, a preserved ecosystem, and a glimpse of the past.

A lodge on the property, once a restaurant and inn, now provides quarters for naturalist workshops. Conservation-concerned visitors can stay for several days, learning about subjects ranging from birding and geology to field sketching, writing, and photography. A small bison herd still lives on the ranch for cultural, historical, and—most importantly—ecological reasons. Their natural grazing habits benefit the land.

"We'd like this to become a place for people to learn about and experience nature," said Mike Gibson, The Nature Conservancy's program director for the Medano-Zapata Ranch project when I visited. Since our conversation, the workshop program at the ranch has blossomed. Scientists are also invited to come and use the ranch as a live location for research projects on animals' grazing habits and their effect on the land, on water management, on the environmental consequences of fire, on invasive species—both plant and anima—and on other ecological processes.

THIS IS NOT JUST ANY WESTERN PRAIRIE. The mountain barriers formed a special world for wildlife, what Nature Conservancy scientist Chris Pague calls a biogeographical island. He explained as we stood on the slopes of the Sangre de Cristos, perhaps not far from where the Folsom hunters scouted for game millennia ago.

"The valley is ringed by peaks that go to 13,000 and 14,000 feet, pretty well isolating species in here from the outside world. Isolation stimulates creativity, so many of the species here developed in ways uniquely their own. There are seven subspecies found only in the valley, including a ground squirrel, a pocket gopher, and an endemic tiger beetle, and we feel they should be preserved," Chris said. "Besides the importance of saving species, we think Americans appreciate seeing the kind of land their ancestors had to work with in settling these areas. Everyone should have the right to hear a buffalo snort."

I heard the buffalo snort in the two weeks I lodged at the Zapata Ranch, adventuring by day on the plains and mountain slopes. I bounced over back roads in a four-wheel-drive with Sharyl Massey, a former Peace Corps volunteer who was serving as the ranch's education director, conveying The Nature Conservancy's philosophy of ecosystem preservation to visitors. "A lot of people here still think the Conservancy is some kind of federal agency," she told me as we walked through a copse of cottonwoods at Sand Creek, where elk often hang out. "We want to show them we're not here to lock up the land. We just want to keep it the way it has always been, for people to learn from and appreciate."

Who couldn't appreciate walking miles on the valley floor, watching pronghorn run in the distance with their rocking-horse gait and mule deer trot away warily on spring-loaded feet, seeing waterbirds fly up from shallow wetlands and a bald eagle crouch over a kill of fresh fish? I hiked a trail one day that led high into the Sangre de Cristos, savoring the scent of piñon and juniper, turning often to gaze with wonder on the widest, flattest valley I have ever beheld. I imagined American explorer Lt. Zebulon Montgomery Pike looking down on the scene for the first time nearly 200 years ago, and I shared his sense that it was "one of the most beautiful and sublime inland prospects ever presented to the eyes of man."

Such scenes could be lost in the clutter of a growing population now discovering this secret corner of the nation. On horseback I helped a rancher outside the Conservancy property herd cattle into higher summer pastures, nudging some of them out of subdivisions that already have sprung up in verdant mountain canyons where elk once dropped their calves.

Gentians open to morning light on the Medano-Zapata Ranch. Despite aridity, 150 species of wildflowers bloom on the valley floor.

A migrating flock of sandhill cranes settles for the night in irrigated shallows of the Monte Vista National Wildlife Refuge.

This is a valley that's beginning to eye its past even as it faces the future, with a growing debate over what effect population growth might have on the majesty of openness. A big slice of open space remains on the Medano and Zapata Ranches, a swatch of yesteryear that the organization hopes will remain unchanged. Ranchers and farmers who might once have seen the Conservancy as a bunch of do-gooding outsiders now admit that both sides share a common goal: preserving a sublime past in the face of a chaotic present. Under the blue slate of a Colorado sky, majestic mountains rising on two sides of the San Luis Valley, the sight of bison grazing and rolling in dust to ward off insects sweeps away the centuries.

Understanding the origins of the huge valley requires mentally sweeping away three miles of vertical earth. Nearly 20 million years ago pressure from the hot mantle in the planet's interior caused the land here to pull apart slowly. Like a tabletop, one slab tilted, its east side pointing up to form the Sangre de Cristos, its west side rotating down 17,000 feet below its original level. Out of the rift created in the separation poured magma in huge volcanic eruptions that filled the underlying valley floor.

The volcanoes cooled and, over millions of years, sand blowing off them and flowing out of them in creeks and rivers helped fill the deep dip between the two ranges. One river flows all the way to Mexico, a journey of 1,885 miles, for in the San Juans are born the headwaters of the Rio Grande. Vegetation covered the valley floor, attracting grazers, and humans followed the grazers. First to appear were the Clovis people—so named for the narrow triangular stone tools they chipped—a little more than 11,000 years ago. Following them were the slightly more advanced Folsom people, whose wanderings over thousands of years littered the valley floor with artifacts.

Anthropologist Dennis Stanford drove me in his geriatric jeep pickup toward a pool called Indian Springs until the sand became too deep for the vehicle. We set off afoot, noting as we left that a bachelor bull bison glowered behind a low dune 40 yards to our right. "One of the hazards of working in this area," muttered Dennis, who has been studying early humans in the valley since 1977. "I hope he doesn't get between us and the truck before we get back." I noted the total lack of trees to climb.

We came to a depression bare of vegetation and blown smooth. "Wind is the great excavator here," said Dennis. "People have been active in the valley for more than 11,000 years, so they had plenty of time to drop things. The wind blows sand over them and then eventually uncovers them again." He hadn't walked ten feet before he bent and picked up a flat rock fragment the size of my thumbnail. "It's a chip off a piece of flint that early man worked to make into some kind of tool." He walked a few more steps and picked up a gray hunk of basalt. "Part of a milling stone used to grind Indian rice grass. Feel how smooth it is on one side from rubbing against another piece of stone in the grinding process?"

A hundred yards beyond the blown-out area we stood before Indian Springs, a clear pool of water 10 yards wide and 50 yards long, with a thin but lively stream flowing out of its lower end. Water shows up in odd places in the otherwise arid valley. Streams flowing off the mountains that surround it seep into the porous soils, then emerge as springs at mid-valley to flow as creeks or gather in shallow lakes.

"See those former streambeds over there?" said Dennis, pointing to banks many

Moonrise over San Luis Lake illuminates four tiers of ecosystems:
wetlands, prairie, desert, and mountain. Annual precipitation averaging 7.5 inches
raises conflicts over water use in the valley, whether for wildlife, recreation, or agriculture.

yards away from the stream. "Pollen studies tell us that the valley was wetter 11,000 years ago, so this stream would have been much bigger." And the grass greener, the grazers more abundant, and the prehistoric hunters active. We returned to the jeep, grateful that the bull had wandered off, and drove to another part of the ranch where Dennis's wife, Pegi Jodry, and two assistants were combing the ground for sites to dig. Both Dennis and Pegi work in the Department of Anthropology of the Smithsonian Institution in Washington, D.C.

Pegi's team had found a mammoth's tooth and a long, fluted stone that was either a broken spear point or part of a knife for flaying meat. They had also found chunks of a grinding stone and had been able to piece together the whole dish-shaped mill, about 7,200 years old. We fanned out, walking with our heads down like philosophers. An assistant spotted a complete arrowhead. Then Dennis found another, still showing perfect notches where it had been bound to the shaft.

An amateur collector would have called it a good day, but Pegi was not pleased. "Complete arrowheads don't help me. They were just lost while the owner was hunting," she complained. "I want to see broken pieces that were tossed aside and replaced while the hunter was relaxing at a camp. That's where I want to dig."

My eyes kept returning to the stone mill, put back together like a puzzle 70 centuries old. Prehistory came alive as I imagined the first Americans kneeling over it to grind Indian rice grass into flour to make rice cakes, about the time the Sumerians were creating the first civilization along the Tigris and Euphrates Rivers.

Written history of the valley began when conquistadores from Mexico entered in the 1580s and claimed it for Spain. The Ute and Comanche there didn't take kindly to being subjects of a distant king. Over 200 years of conflict the Spanish expeditions never established control north of New Mexico, although they managed to name some of the major features. The mountains were named in 1719 by the Spanish explorer Antonio Valver de y Cosio, who was so overcome as he gazed at the hues of red shared by a sunrise and the red-tinted, snowy peaks, he supposedly uttered a fervent *Sangre de Cristo!*—the Blood of Christ! A Spanish missionary named Francisco Torres looked down from a hill and, moved by the beauty of the broad valley, called it San Luis, for the patron saint of his home village of Seville. Days later, Torres was killed during an Indian attack.

Plenty of blood colored the valley well into the 19th century as Native Americans, beaver-trapping mountain men, and soldiers of the young United States all vied for use of the mountain-rimmed land. Although the U.S. wrested it from its southern neighbor in the 1848 Mexican War, the first non-Indian residents were Spanish-speaking settlers out of the south. Their influence can still be seen in the adobe architecture of some communities and in the names of towns such as Saguache, Del Norte, and Alamosa.

Only Alamosa has grown substantially—to a population of 12,000, which swells to near 15,000 when Adams State College is in session. Although those early Hispanic settlements were the first in Colorado and Anglos later moved in to establish large farms and ranches, the San Luis Valley has lagged behind the rest of the state and remains its poorest region. Apparently that horseshoe of mountains has formed an economic as well as a biological island. A standing joke in the valley goes: "If you want to make a million dollars here, bring two million with you when you come."

Even that doesn't always work. Millions went toward making a theme park on the valley floor before the scheme ran into bugs, wind blasts, and love of bison.

In 1989 a New York architect named Hisayoshi (Hisa) Ota and a Japanese partner bought the Medano and Zapata Ranches with a scheme to create a huge recreation area, including four golf courses. In addition to business from Americans, they hoped the courses would draw avid Japanese golfers from abroad. Japan's economy was flying high and golf had grown enormously popular there, but courses were both crowded and expensive. Japanese groups seeking a vacation on the links could golf more cheaply in the San Luis Valley than they could at home, including the cost of a chartered flight from Tokyo.

Unfortunately, the development partners weren't familiar with the length of valley winters, which left only three months of golfing weather. In spring the wind rattles trousers and loosens caps, and by summer the mosquitoes, gnats, and horseflies grow hungry. After building one course, which lost money steadily, Hisa's partner wanted out. Hisa, who left Japan at 17 and has lived in the U.S. now a quarter century, fell in love with the valley.

"When I first came here, I thought the place was a wasteland," the fortyish architect told me, "but I was busy with architectural projects and just went along with the deal. As I spent more time here I began to appreciate how this 'wasteland' could support so many plants and animals. I was especially fascinated by the bison, which seemed so prehistoric and so suitable to the land.

"I had been living in a loft on Fifth Avenue where I couldn't even see the sky. Out here there was plenty of sky. The few lights visible at night reminded me of the lights of Japanese fishing boats at sea, and the whole valley seemed like a vast ocean of land."

Hisa took over the property, abandoning the plan for a recreation mecca and trying instead to operate the ranches and the one golf course in an environmentally friendly way. With no experience in ranching and with the golf course a continuing financial drain, he felt he could not do environmental justice to the land. After visiting another Nature Conservancy property and seeing how they managed it, he sold the two ranches to The Nature Conservancy at four million dollars under market value.

Hisa and his wife, Kris, built a house on the slopes of the Sangre de Cristo mountains, overlooking the valley. They bottle-raised a bison heifer calf that had been abandoned by its mother. Amelia now runs to them like a 1,500-pound puppy dog and hangs out near the kitchen window, where she can hear their voices. "We enjoy the bison, the beautiful sunsets, and the bugling of the elk for what they are: natural beauty that we hope will last forever," said the man who once planned to turn the prairie into a giant resort.

Some 300 head of cattle still grazing in separate pastures may be phased out someday to give bison the run of the ranch. For now, the cows remain, a source of income and a subject of grazing research. A carefully monitored herd might answer questions that have gained importance as environmental awareness increases: How many cows can graze together, sharing a given area, before the plant life and the wild creatures sharing it are damaged?

But the bulk of the sprawling ranch is given back to the bison. Their wandering area may double if the Baca Ranch, another 100,000 acres adjoining the Medano-Zapata to the north, is added to federal lands. Overseeing the herd is the Conservancy's ranch manager Tom Bragg, a young veterinarian who grew up in Nebraska. Although fences keep the humped herbivores on ranch property, the animals wander a range so large that despite its flatness, they sometimes must be located by a flight in Hisa's small plane. "It's genetically programmed into bison to eat and walk, eat and walk," said Tom, "because for thousands of years they ate and walked from Texas to North Dakota in spring and back again in the fall. Cattle, on the other hand, will stay in one place as long as the grass is good there."

The bison herd now consists of about 450 cows and 50 bulls, roaming freely over the property, fenced in only on its perimeter. You see the young bulls in the off-breeding season standing alone on the prairie like the backs of old nickels, seemingly nursing some grudge against the world. Could they but know what symbolic figures they cut, standing into wind that ruffles their wooly humps, sending the imagination hurtling back two centuries, when their forebears blackened the prairies, it might help their dispositions. But it doesn't, so the best advice is, steer clear of bachelor bulls.

As Hisa said, the bison seem exactly in their element, but their wanderings sometimes bring them up against a scene that could have been pulled from northern Africa. In the northeast corner of the valley lie the Great Sand Dunes, a national monument that was approved by Congress as a national park in the year 2000.

You could be in the Sahara when you climb on the graceful beige drifts and, in fact, in the 30 square miles they encompass you climb on dunes greater than those found in that great African desert. Up to 750 feet high, they rank as the tallest dunes in North America and the second tallest in the world, exceeded only by those in China's Gobi. The winds keep changing their shape at will, building new peaks and carving new cornices overnight. Some 300,000 visitors come every year to clamber on the dunes, looking from the valley below like creepy-crawlies on a giant anthill.

I JOINED THEM LATE ONE AFTERNOON, determined to make it to the top of the tallest sandy ridge. Climbing any steep incline is tough, made tougher when, with every step forward, your foot slips back halfway to where it started. Even more discouraging, I picked the wrong peak and climbed halfway up its steep slopes before realizing that to my left was one even higher. Retreating, I crossed a deep trough and then struggled on all fours up a steep slope I had just slid down easily. Finally I trudged to the top of one of the world's biggest sandpiles.

Punished for my efforts by a 40-mph wind, I relished a quick look at the ocean of prairie below before heading back down, sand peppering my bare legs like tiny buck-shot. Ascent had been laborious but descent was a joy—giant strides that plunged each foot ankle-deep in sand and put me back on the valley floor in 15 minutes. On the way I passed youngsters tobogganing down the steep slopes on flattened pieces of box cardboard.

This is one facility run by the National Park Service where visitors are encouraged to deface the terrain. Park rangers urge them to write their names in huge letters in the sand, leave footprints, break off sharp edges, and slide down pristine slopes, because overnight winds will wipe the slate clean by next morning. No littering, of course, because like the arrowheads on the valley floor, what the wind covers one day it may uncover the next.

One bit of major defacing resulted in federal protection for the sand dunes. Early in the 20th century, mining companies were plumbing the sand for gold, getting about an ounce for every ton they processed but gouging large dents in the drifts. A local philan-thropic women's group protested, and in 1932 President Hoover declared the area Great Sand Dunes National Monument.

Barren though the dunes may seem, they are home to tenacious life-forms, some proving useful to science. Grasses, scurfpeas, and prairie sunflowers have adapted to life in the shifting sands. Kangaroo rats that may never take a drink live off moisture in the seeds, plants, and insects they eat. Six insects found here live nowhere else on earth. Among them is the Great Sand Dunes tiger beetle, a voracious little predator so quick that it out-runs its own eyesight.

"When the sun is out, but before it gets too hot, the beetle comes out of its burrow and looks for red ants and sand mites," Phyllis Pineda told me at the dunes. Study-ing the tiger beetle for her master's thesis at Colorado State University, she spies on the little speedsters with binoculars that bring them into tight focus. "When it sees one, it dashes forward so fast that its multifaceted eyes lose sight of the prey, requiring it to stop and refocus. So it dashes, stops, dashes, stops, until it catches the prey, rips it to shreds, and eats it.

"We tend to worry about charismatic megafauna, but if a little creature like this disappears it may be the first sign that something is wrong with the ecosystem."

Another dune bug is so adaptable that some of its members are becoming astro-nauts. College undergraduates Rachel Scott and Katie Montanaro were collecting darkling beetles to see how zero gravity in the International Space Station might affect their ability to function and reproduce. The beetles' hardiness in a valley with temperature changes that can range from minus 50 degrees to 91 degrees Fahrenheit made them prime candidates. The two young women referred to their collection as "the astronaut corps" and tested each on a tiny treadmill to determine which were suitable for the rigors of space flight.

Park director Fred Bunch gave me a lesson in dune mechanics, driving me in a fat-tired pickup to Medano Creek between the dunes and the Sangre de Cristo Mountains. "Southwest winds blow sand off the San Juan Mountains and across the valley floor," he said. "The Rio Grande has also meandered through the valley for centuries, depositing sand that later blows here. When the sand reaches the northeast corner of the valley, it can't make it over the steep ridges, so it piles up at their feet. The wind reflecting off the mountains

Blooming rabbitbrush gleams in a late sun. Developers once planned to convert much of the world's largest inhabited alpine valley into a theme park. Purchase of the Medano and Zapata Ranches and 100,000 acres of grazing rights has allowed The Nature Conservancy to preserve natural plant and animal communities.

curls down, reverses direction, and blows up the backs of the dunes, creating these steep cliffs. Some of the sand falls into Medano Creek, which transports it around to the front, where it is recycled onto the dunes. So it's a constant process of sand moving and changing the shape of the dunes. The Utes used to call this area Sewampowa-u-uvay—place where the land goes back and forth."

Farther up the slope of the Sangre de Cristos, I saw scars on ponderosa pines made by the Ute more than a century ago. "They peeled big pieces of bark off one side and used it for food and medicine," said Fred, as we stood by one large tree with a weathered bare spot nearly ten feet up the trunk and a yard wide. "The cambium layer tastes faintly of butterscotch. We've tested it and found it contains large amounts of calcium. A Ute elder told me that when a tribal member had a stomachache, they would have them lean against a freshly peeled trunk for a time to make them feel better."

Carbon-dating the wood of the bare spot and comparing it to the outer layer of remaining bark can determine the year of harvest. The one we stood by had been peeled in 1860 and was still healthy. "They never girdled a tree, knowing that would kill it," said Fred.

Farther up the slope we saw other markings in aspens along Medano Creek— scratches made by the claws of a black bear reaching high. The last grizzly in the valley was shot in the 1960s. We passed several exquisitely engineered dams built by beavers, whose ancestors drew white trappers to the valley. At one bend in the creek we surprised two Rocky Mountain sheep rams burdened by thick horns curling off their heads and trailed by a young lamb hanging out with the big boys. The trio scrambled back to the safety of the high ground from which they had come for a drink.

As in much of the arid West, the availability of water governs all activities in the San Luis Valley. Although an average of only seven and a half inches of rain falls annually, the basin remains green because of two layers of underground aquifers. The upper layer includes mountain runoff that gradually seeps into the sand and becomes groundwater, known as the unconfined aquifer. It often reemerges at low spots in the valley when it reaches a level of impermeable clay, creating shallow lakes and springs. Such a reemergence, for example, created Indian Springs. Below the clay lies a deeper reservoir, known as the confined aquifer, which also contributes water to the upper level. Tinkering with the sub-surface water systems has altered the face of the San Luis Valley.

IN THE 1930s, A FEUD AROSE BETWEEN Colorado, New Mexico, and Texas, all of whom wanted the Rio Grande's water for irrigation. Before the feud turned into a water war, the federal government stepped in and negotiated an agreement called the Rio Grande Compact of 1938. Colorado promised the other two states a measurable amount of Rio Grande flow, and they in turn promised to let a certain amount pass beyond them into Mexico.

But with so much water being diverted for agricultural irrigation in the San Luis Valley, Colorado fell short of its guaranteed flow and created a water debt. To pay it, the state legislature in 1972 approved the Closed Basin Project, in which Rio Grande shortfalls would be made up with water pulled from the deep confined aquifer. Pumping from the aquifer lowered the water table, drying up some of the shallow lakes used by waterfowl. In compensation, water from the Rio Grande was diverted to other areas—creating the Blanca Wetlands and the Alamosa and Monte Vista National Wildlife Refuges. Aquatically, Peter was robbed to pay Paul, and then Peter was repaid with a different currency.

Throughout the valley some 230,000 acres of wetlands provide food and cover for thousands of waterbirds, songbirds, beavers, elk, deer, and coyotes. In March, 27,000 sandhill cranes come to Alamosa during their migration northward to Idaho and Montana. As nesting areas for wild ducks, the refuges rank as one of the highest production areas in the U.S. More acres of wetlands exist now in the valley than before the Closed Basin Project, but the trade-off is not the same, says Nature Conservancy scientist Chris Pague. "Sure, you get some popular species that everyone can see and appreciate," he told me, "but the small species that made use of the natural pools, such as the northern leopard frog, can't make it in the artificial ones. We're interested in preserving all biodiversity, not just a few highly visible ones."

Ralph Curtis, Jr., general manager of the Rio Grande Water Conservation District, admits that environmental considerations have gained influence in recent years. "In 1973, when the Closed Basin Project was approved, economics dictated everything that happened to this land and science had little to do with it," he told me at his Alamosa office. "By 1981 people were beginning to question whether you should tinker with nature on such a big scale, but the project was already in motion so construction [of deep wells and canals] continued. I doubt that we could even get permission for such a project today."

Around the turn of this century, a private scheme to sell the valley's deep water to urban communities sparked a storm of protest from ranchers, farmers, and environmentalists. A group called the Stockman's Water Company planned a series of deep wells on the Baca Ranch at the north end of the valley to pump water from the confined aquifer and pipe it over to Colorado Springs. Lowering the deep aquifer, others feared, could dry up the entire valley. Part of the ranch may be added to the newly created Great Sand Dunes National Park, which would remove the threat of water loss.

The valley's natural hydrology created the unique phenomenon of deserts and wetlands existing side by side, each with its own plant and animal community. Some of the last and best of the small natural lakes that once dotted the valley lie in the northwest corner, miles from the Medano-Zapata Ranch. Spring showers and snowmelt from the mountains annually fill the Mishak Lakes. Before most turn to cracked checkerboards of dried mud in summer, they are used by a galaxy of wildlife. The Nature Conservancy has bought 3,000 acres that include the lakes to preserve their natural biodiversity.

Chris Pague, Sharyl Massey, and I walked several miles from lake to lake one June day when most of them still held water. A few yards away from their shores we crunched over a near-desert of mineralized hardpan where little grew but rabbitbrush, greasewood, and a few grasses. Even here, evidence of life appeared: pronghorn droppings, a cottontail dashing off, a ground squirrel skittering to cover.

Approaching one of the lakes, a marsh hawk rose out of the tall grass and ducks and teal exploded off the water. A Wilson's phalarope hovered just beyond arm's reach, sure sign of a nest nearby. Yellow-headed blackbirds clung to reeds, and we counted six black-crowned night-herons. At another isolated pool just inches deep, two American avocets dive-bombed us and, when that didn't drive us away, both alighted in the shallows and began broken-wing acts designed to lure us after them. Out of the corner of my eye I spied a downy chick scuttling through saltgrass in the opposite direction.

The appreciation of natural ecosystems continues to grow in the San Luis Valley. As more outsiders discover the mountain-rimmed haven and as subdivisions burgeon, environmentalists and descendants of pioneers find themselves in unlikely agreement about preserving the quality of life. "The idea of some stiff-necked old cowmen I have worked for being forced to cozy up to some ex-hippy with tree-hugging tendencies to protect a ranch sort of boggles my mind," wrote longtime farmer Vess Quinlan in a valley publication in 1997. "But that's my prediction and I'm sticking to it. It will be the price for our survival. We will have to pay a lot more attention to stewardship."

Mike Spearman hated seeing subdivisions creep into a quiet canyon of the La Garita Mountains, part of the San Juan range. The owners of the ranch he managed had sold off some small plots as they felt the pinch of ranching costs, and they planned to sell even more to a developer. Mike introduced them to the Conservancy, which helped them set up conservation easements that forbid development while giving them tax advantages. The Nature Conservancy recently bought 1,700 more canyon acres used by elk for winter calving.

We rode past some of the new houses as we rounded up cattle to head them into summer pastures in the mountains. "You can't blame people for wanting a nice home site, but it sure changes the place," said Mike. "Some let the cattle graze on their property, which entitles them to an agricultural exemption. But others fence their plot to put a couple of horses on it and graze the vegetation down to nothing, or leave only the undesirable stuff. The deer, elk, and mountain sheep that used to use this canyon now have one less place to go. And sediment washes off the road that had to be built up here and affects stream life.

"But, what's done's done," he said with a shrug and with the same acceptance with which he's adjusted to losing one hand and a part of another to a stick of dynamite that misfired on the ranch. ("Having three fingers on one hand and a clamp on the other didn't slow him down any," said one of his cowhands.)

"People like to live along a nice stream with a little acreage. We just have to be careful that it doesn't happen too much," said Mike. "More and more landowners are taking out conservation easements. People here have an appreciation of the life they have, living off the land and letting wildlife use it as well. They don't want to lose that just by selling out to a developer for a bundle of cash."

With two ranch hands, we urged 300 bawling animals out of the canyon and up a trail to higher ground. Whoever thinks driving cows means casually trailing after them, yodeling cowboy tunes, never met the horned hooligan on my side of the bunch. She persisted in leading others off the trail, up steep slopes and into stickery brush and stockades of aspens, where I had to follow numerous times on a blue-collar horse named Fancy. I banged my knee painfully on a tree trunk as I razzed the cow back to the herd, calling her names unrelated to her lineage. After 20 yards of docile plodding, into the brush she'd go again, seeking some mountainside nirvana of her own dull imagination. The tiresome tag game was fair payment for a day on horseback in the piñon-juniper forests studded by rounded granite spires, under a bowl of clearest blue sky.

Maybe economic isolation was the best thing that could have happened here, says Sally Harper, administrator of Los Caminos Antiguas (The Historic Route), a local organization that celebrates the rich story of the San Luis Valley. "Maybe now we can develop more slowly and not make the same mistakes of other areas," she told me in her Alamosa office. "A lot of people here want to preserve the viewshed and the lifestyle, while helping the community develop." In addition to sustainable ranching and farming, she said, the valley can sell its history and natural beauty to outside visitors. "Some of our old villages along the historic route are just like old Mexico. There's wildlife to be seen, the Great Sand Dunes, hiking in the mountains, and rides on the old narrow-gauge railroad behind a steam locomotive to old gold-mining towns."

And there are wide open spaces, where the buffalo roam.

The Nature Conservancy explores ways for the now-combined Medano-Zapata Ranch to sustain itself, whether by holding workshops and conferences or by leasing land to local ranchers. Staff members conduct ranch tours throughout the summer, giving the public opportunities to visit this special place. Aware that local involvement is essential for success, Conservancy representatives work together with local people and organizations. "We have gained the support of opinion leaders, community members, ranchers, and farmers throughout the valley," says Audrey Wolk, marketing director for the Colorado chapter of the Conservancy. "We do this not just to ensure mission success but to ensure that the local way of life is safeguarded."

A wealth of special quiet and clarity seems encompassed in this mountain-rimmed Eden. Nearly every night I spent at the Zapata Ranch I stepped outside at some point and was struck by the milky cover of abundant stars and the enormous silence. Fred Bunch at Great Sand Dunes had told me that sound monitors were once placed in the valley and overnight they failed to register anything, not even crickets, because the coolness kept the insects still.

Quiet lands rich in natural wonders grow harder and harder to find, at the very time that they gain importance in our noisome lives. Where they still exist, they smooth out the frayed edges of harried minds and rearm us for the mental assaults of a modern world. Silence and beauty speak eloquently of our need to keep the last great places intact forever. ▪

Bison graze in the San Luis Valley, a scene frozen in time. Scattered artifacts reveal human presence in the valley for thousands of years, hunting earlier herds. The preserve allows glimpses into the West's natural past and research into the effects of grazing on the future.

western
united states
portfolio

WE CALL IT THE WILD WEST and speak of its wide open spaces, but civilization now presses in on natural communities where yucca blooms under marbled skies. The less populated half of the United States still offers opportunities to save large areas and the original species living in them.

A SEA OF tallgrass, often dotted with bison, can still be experienced in Kansas's eastern Flint Hills, on a huge preserve known as Konza Prairie. Spared from plows because the steep slopes and shallow limestone soils were unsuitable for cultivation, the 8,616-acre property appears much as Native Americans knew it and white settlers first saw it. Grasses dominate: big bluestem, little bluestem, Indian grass, and switchgrass, accompanied by buckbrush, sumac, and hardwoods alongside the streams. The preserve owners, The Nature Conservancy and nearby Kansas State University, operate Konza as a field research station to promote better understanding of prairie processes. A hundred ecological research projects may be underway at any given time. Visitors can hike trails of three, five, or six miles in length—near but separate from the bison that are often visible on a distant hill—to view the heartland as it once existed.

THE VALUE OF a river in the desert can be measured in the gold of Mexican poppies (right) alongside the San Pedro River. For 150 miles this sliver of life flows through the parched Sonoran landscape, north from Mexico into the United States. The combination of low desert, high mountains, and watered riparian zone collects a mother lode of biodiversity, including the Colorado hairstreak butterfly (far right). Birds moving with the seasons follow this watery thread and some nest along it, making the yardwide stream, with 385 species, the most dense and diverse avian harbor in the nation. The mix of 83 different mammals in the valley exceeds that of

RISING OUT OF the Gila National Forest, the Gila River at its headwaters splashes over boulders through a deep canyon. The most diverse deciduous woodland in New Mexico is fed by this, the state's last major free-flowing river. Nine imperiled fish species find a home in the stream, and in riparian forests of sycamores, oaks, and rare cottonwood willows clusters one of the U.S.'s densest songbird breeding populations. The woodlands also offer sanctuary for birds migrating to and from Central America. Thousand-year-old Native American ruins and pottery lie along its banks.

Downstream from the river's steeper beginnings, The Nature Conservancy operates a thousand-acre Gila Riparian Preserve, restoring agricultural lands to former plant communities and attempting compatible farming methods. In private agricultural areas, the Conservancy works with farmers and ranchers to find common solutions aimed at saving the river.

A BULL ELK with antlers still sheathed in summer velvet grazes near the Gibbon River, a powerful symbol of the largest intact wild ecosystem in the continental United States. Although millions have visited the famous 2.2-million-acre national park, the Greater Yellowstone system encompasses 18 million acres, both public and private lands. Some 30,000 elk and the last herds of free-ranging bison roam its wilds, preyed upon by grizzlies and reintroduced wolves. Foothills and river corridors harbor unique plant communities.

Despite its massive size, Yellowstone faces threats that nibble at its effectiveness as a protector of natural systems. Planned mining could affect the water. Petroleum developers want to build more roads. Vacation homes bring human presence and interrupt the seasonal migration of wildlife. The Nature Conservancy works with others to protect this huge chunk of the West.

THE FUTURE once looked as dark as the
storm clouds behind these oaks along the
last major undammed river of the Sierra
Nevada's western slope. Much of the
80-mile-long Cosumnes had been leveed
to create agricultural lands, and the suburbs of nearby Sacramento threatened to
spill onto its banks. In 1984 The Nature
Conservancy bought 85 acres of virgin
oaks to create the Cosumnes River Preserve, now grown to 37,042 acres with
both public and private partners. In the
Cosumnes River Project, levees have been
breached and rice and bean fields
restored to oak savannas and wetlands.
Some 80,000 birds of 150 species now
winter in new wetlands, and riparian
forests of willow, cottonwood, and oak
have been reestablished by hand-planting
and natural processes. Rice operations
compatible with wildlife have been
encouraged, some showing a greater
profit than traditional methods, demon-
strating that both people and wildlife can
be served along a beautiful river.

FOR CENTURIES the Williamson River meandered across a 12-square-mile delta before emptying into Klamath Lake. The slow journey cleaned sediments from the water and created wetlands that nourished millions of waterfowl. The Lost River sucker and the short-nosed sucker, two fish that were once a major food source for Native Americans, took refuge in the marshes and matured in the lake.

With the diking and channeling of the river for agriculture, wetlands disappeared and water quality deteriorated in Klamath Lake, one of America's largest freshwater bodies of water. The sucker fish became endangered. The numbers of waterfowl diminished by more than half, but they still constitute one of the largest concentrations in the United States. More than a hundred of the vertebrate species in the Klamath Basin are now rare or imperiled. On a 7,000-acre preserve, The Nature Conservancy and numerous public and private partners are re-creating some of these important wetlands by breaching dikes, reconnecting the river to the adjacent wetlands, and reestablishing the life-sustaining course of these waters.

WATERS NEAR Gull Island boil with murres and gulls in a bay so rich it has been designated a National Estuarine Research Reserve. Upwellings from the nearby Gulf of Alaska swirl nutrients into this marine cornucopia, supporting runs of five species of salmon, visits by hundreds of thousands of seabirds and migrating shorebirds, and breeding activities by sea otters, Steller's sea lions, and humpback whales. The adjacent watershed holds bald eagles, brown and black bears, and moose.

Despite protection as a research reserve, state critical area, and shorebird reserve, the glacier-bright bay now feels the impact of civilization. Few planning requirements exist on its shores, and residentialconstruction has been extensive. Logging leaks in sediment, and ships from an oil refinery at the north end have spilled poisonous by-products. The Nature Conservancy monitors the condition of the bay and the surrounding watershed to note changes that might spur protective action.

ASIA

*Holy place to Buddhists, gatepost
to scenic splendor, Kawagebo Peak rears
more than 20,000 feet above the clouds
in China's rugged Yunnan Province.*

*Steep gorges cast shadows on a glinting river
in China's Yunnan Province.*

in search of
shangri-la

Nothing stamps wildness on an area
like the cry of the wolf.
Short barks followed by long baritone wails
played the perfect predawn concert
for this remote valley in China's Yunnan Province.
I lay awake in my hut for a few moments,
relishing a sound seldom heard in the 21st century.

As THE LIGHT GREW and the last of the calls trailed away, I pulled on fleece and stepped into October. Before me lay a green meadow dotted by trees and touched here and there by fingers of fog. Twin streams flowed down each side of the meadow, one of the streams crossing in front of me to join with the other.

Towering over the view at the far end of the meadow, the highest peaks of the snow-covered Meili Snow Range already gleamed with rays of sunlight that would not reach the valley floor for hours. No human has ever conquered Meili's ramparts. When a joint team of Chinese and Japanese climbers tried in 1991, local Buddhists, who believe its 22,100-foot heights fit only for gods, prayed for failure. An avalanche killed 17 climbers.

I walked into the center of this amphitheater and slowly turned in all directions. On two sides rose tree-covered mountains that harbored deer, wild sheep, Asiatic brown bears, snow leopards, and the wolves I'd heard. At one end the white-robed massif of Kawagebo stood sentinel over the pleasant valley like a lighthouse over a safe harbor. At the other end lay the unobtrusive village of Yubeng, a dozen dwellings of wood and stone nestled against a tree-green ridge, the fourth wall around this Shangri-la.

A huge silence hung over the vastness. Only donkey trails enter the valley and, while villagers were probably stirring in their homes or milking their yaks, no movement could be seen. The thatched houses and rock-walled grain fields around them sat frozen, as if on a canvas from the age of enlightenment. I tried to saturate my senses with the view, hoping it could be recalled later to combat noise, haste, and visual clutter on the outside.

Shangri-la—When British author James Hilton gave that name to an idealized, mountain-locked valley in the Far East, in his 1933 novel *Lost Horizon,* the word leaped into the English language. He depicted a utopia where humble people lived centuries-long, stress-free lives in a land of plenty. The image appealed to Westerners beset by a Great Depression and threatened by the possibility of a second Great War.

Today we celebrate our Shangri-las as refreshment for the human psyche in a world becoming more crowded, more frenetic, more detached from the natural environment. In the explosion of human population, areas virtually unaffected by development have shrunk to a precious few. Where they exist, monumental efforts are required to keep them unspoiled. In Yunnan, The Nature Conservancy teamed with the Chinese in 1998 to help direct the tide of tourism that could otherwise swamp the province's scenic simplicity and threaten its biodiversity.

With its pushed-up mountains and deep river-cut gorges, Yunnan Province in southern China has walled out change longer than most corners of the world, including much of China itself. When tectonically drifting India rammed into the belly of Asia millennia ago and partly burrowed under it, the long, slow collision wrinkled the Himalaya and lifted the entire Tibetan plateau. Just as a great ship sends out bow waves while knifing through the sea, the prow of the subcontinent also pushed up bow waves of rock hundreds of miles to the east, a series of mountain ridges that curve gently southward. Snowmelt draining off the high Tibetan plateau runs between these ridges, cutting their valleys even deeper and forming four of Asia's great rivers, the Salween, the Mekong, the Yangtze, and a branch of the Irrawaddy called the Dulong.

Pressure and gravity have created a landscape so precipitous that the Japanese bypassed most of it in their invasion of China in World War II. The safe haven gave U.S. cargo planes and the famous Flying Tigers places to land as they flew over the Himalaya—"the hump"—out of India and across Burma to support Chinese and Allied troops. Tribal groups sequestered by vertical rock have kept their customs as the rest of the world has grown homogeneous, so that today half of China's distinct ethnic minorities live in Yunnan.

So steep are Yunnan's gorges that rockslides frequently erase sections of roads that bulldozers and dynamite have carved into the mountainsides. With transportation uncertain, industry and residential growth are stalemated, and the northwestern reaches of Yunnan have remained a land recognized internationally for its extraordinary biodiversity, primarily because three of the world's four types of biogeographic domains meet here—humid tropical, humid temperate, and polar—a confluence that occurs in few other places on Earth. On northwest Yunnan's high slopes grow 7,000 plant species, including three-quarters of Tibet's traditional medicinal herbs and nearly half of China's. More than 30 rare and endangered animal species live here, including the snow leopard, the golden monkey, the red panda, and the black-necked crane. Of China's 1,300 bird species, 450 are found in Yunnan, and out of the 9,700 bird species found worldwide, 4 percent can be seen here. In dozens of side valleys, the pressures of the 20th century bypassed villages nestled in bucolic backwaters.

Now the detour is disappearing. China's emergence from a planned economy into a free market has created a moneyed class that seeks vacations in glorious scenery. City dwellers from Kunming, Dali, and distant Shanghai venture onto the cliffside roads armed with cameras to record waterfalls and snow-covered peaks, and to witness tribespeople in bright costumes. Northwest Yunnan has become China's Alaska, where well-heeled visitors can feel like explorers by day and sleep in a warm bed at night after a hot shower and a restaurant meal. With the advent of traffic, crowds, and commercialism, tourism threatens to violate Yunnan's virgin charms.

In an agreement unthinkable in the political tensions of the recent past, The Nature Conservancy acts as an advisor to the Yunnan provincial government in an endeavor known as the Yunnan Great Rivers Project. In an area the size of West Virginia, the Chinese and the Conservancy hope to create a way of life that will save the wildness, the beauty, the species, and the distinct cultures, and improve the lives of the people as well.

"The first phase was helping prepare an extensive conservation plan that took into account the biological and cultural diversity, the threats to it, and the conservation activities needed to maintain it," said Ed Norton, a Washington lawyer and environmentalist who heads the Conservancy effort in Yunnan. "Phase two becomes more precise, working in partnership with government at all levels—provincial, village, regional, county, and national—to devise action plans in specific communities." More tourists will pour into Yunnan Province, but The Nature Conservancy and the Chinese are banking that the hard-earned yuan they spend will feed economic benefit to the region without trampling its beauty.

Sun spotlights the checkerboard fields and scattered houses of a mountain-rimmed valley in Yunnan. Seclusion in remote valleys

may have inspired James Hilton's fictional account of Shangri-la in the 1930s novel Lost Horizon.

Light rain does not deter a Tibetan woman, member of one of the larger ethnic groups in Yunnan Province. With ice-covered

peaks walling out change, half of China's distinct ethnic minorities still follow their traditional customs in remote Yunnan.

WITH THE FUTURE STILL IN DOUBT, the wave of the present can already be seen around the city of Lijiang, located near the point where the Yangtze first loops to reverse direction on its long, winding journey to the China Sea. The clean, bright city of just under 80,000 lies on a vast plain below a towering white giant, Yulongxue Shan, or Jade Dragon Snow Range. The perpetual snows on Jade Dragon send down cascades of cold, fresh water, some of it running directly through the canals of the city.

Virtually leveled by an earthquake in 1996, Lijiang remade itself within a couple of years, raising modern buildings under rigid seismic codes. Restored as well was the low-profile Old Town known as Gu Cheng, designated a World Heritage site by UNESCO in 1997. Its tile-roof houses and narrow streets crisscrossed by canals strike an accent of quaintness popular with both foreign and Chinese tourists, who jam its narrow cobblestone streets day and night. The row houses sport boutiques selling T-shirts, wall hangings, embroidery, jade carvings, and jewelry. Busy restaurants line the canals, and patrons chat animatedly, quaff beer, and lever in rice with their chopsticks as water lily blossoms float by. Quaintness sells, the Chinese have found, and so does spectacular scenery, now that a new leisure class has lifted its eyes from the hardscrabble existence of yesterday's socialist revolution.

Tourism development began in the Lijiang area before The Nature Conservancy became involved in 1998. Outside the city, at the foot of Jade Dragon Snow Range, an entire tourist village is sprouting, with hotels, restaurants, pony rides, and a 36-hole golf course. The construction is planned and financed by a consortium of companies backed by foreign and domestic money and overseen by the national government. Attempts at careful development have been made—a cable car climbing to mountain heights is hidden from valley view and commercial development is limited to a four-and-a-half-mile area.

With hundreds of Chinese I rode up to the glaciers and near the peaks of Jade Dragon. The views of snow and raw, jagged rock were already above the clouds, but ahead lay a zigzagging stretch of wooden stairs, leading to a final high platform for sneakered mountaineers. On the stairs moved an army of scenery-minded Chinese, trudging bent over and weary in the thin oxygen, resembling Mao Zedong's forces on the Long March. The highest platform stood at 14,500 feet, some 4,000 feet beneath one of the range's highest peaks. Off came coats and out came cameras, pointed at men raising their fists in triumph against an alpine backdrop and women posing like Armani models in form-fitting tank tops and tight jeans.

The gondola is one of three mechanized means of assailing the heights near Lijiang. After descending again to breathable air, I boarded a ski lift a few miles away for a ride to a high plateau called Yun Shan Ping, or Spruce Meadow—a mesmerizing stage with a tragic past. In the meadow a scattering of cattle and Tibetan ponies cropped at a green carpet of perhaps a hundred acres, surrounded by high conifers. A late afternoon sun highlighted the snowy peaks beyond the trees, and scattered clouds broke the rays into brilliant shafts of light, one of which spotlighted the center of the meadow like a message from God.

To this scene of ethereal splendor young lovers used to climb for joint suicides when their desires were about to be thwarted by arranged marriages to others. Today, romance dictates the weddings of Chinese young people as it does in most countries of the world,

Rhododendron brighten a cheerful stream in Yunnan. Snowmelt draining from the Tibetan plateau feeds four of Asia's great rivers in Yunnan—the Salween, Mekong, Yangtze, and a branch of the Irrawaddy. Pushed-up mountains and deep-cut gorges have limited human impacts, leaving a concentration of rare plants and animals.

but the last couple to hang together from the branches of these stately trees made their sad ascent to Spruce Meadow in the 20th century. The haunting outdoor cathedral of sun-shot beauty cried out for respectful silence, but the air was rent by the calls of visitors wanting to hear their echoes and the *thweep* of guards' whistles scolding those who left the board-walk to tread on the grass.

Visitors to the Jade Dragon recreation area pay 45 yuan (more than five dollars) to enter the recreation area, a similar fee for the ski lift to the meadow, and 110 yuan (nearly fifteen dollars) to ride the gondola to the snowy ramparts. With 1.25 million visitors coming to the Jade Dragon recreation area in the year 2000 and their numbers steadily rising, tourism will soon be the major player in the Lijiang economy.

"We believe it will promote other sectors, such as agriculture and flower growing, to feed and amuse the visitors," Wang Yun, director of the consortium developing the area, told me. "We hope Jade Dragon can be a model for tourist development throughout the province."

The onslaught of more than a million visitors a year bothers some science minds. From the platform atop the range, I had glimpsed on a distant slope the tracks of mountain sheep, stitching patterns across the snow. There are rumors of snub-nosed monkeys, red pandas, and snow leopards living on the Jade Dragon Snow Range, a nature preserve one-tenth the size of America's Yellowstone National Park. Three times during my visit to the heights, local hawkers offered me beautiful fur hats made of red panda fur. When the ani-mal's threatened status was pointed out, the response was always the same: "No problem, this hat belonged to my grandfather and was handed down to me." Sure it was.

WHAT EFFECT MIGHT HEAVY TOURISM have on species living here, when there are no actual inventories of plant and animal life on the slopes? This sort of question perenni-ally concerns those working with The Nature Conservancy.

No such questions existed when NATIONAL GEOGRAPHIC correspondent Joseph Rock posed in a hat of red panda fur in the 1920s and 1930s. For 27 years, Rock lived in Yunnan Province, collecting rare herbs, photographing and writing about the area, and mounting expeditions into uncharted territories. For many of those years Rock lived in the village of Nguluko, at the foot of the Jade Dragon, among an ethnic group known as the Naxi (Nah-zhee).

A people related to the Tibetans, slightly darker and often taller than the domi-nant Han Chinese, the Naxi are distinctive as well for their cultural achievements. Their pic-tographic language is believed to be one of the oldest still in use (although understood now only by shamans). A performing Naxi orchestra uses instruments that date to ancient times. In the Naxi village called Baishi, near Nguluko, a small group performs daily for tourist dona-tions. The ragged sound emanating from one-stringed violins, hand-carved piccolos, and the ululation of a woman soloist is best appreciated from an anthropological standpoint.

Baishi beckons the tourist yuan in other ways, with stalls for selling trinkets and re-created pictographs. The seller of these picture stories, offered as wall hangings, interpreted one for me that represented the saying, "There's no distance too far for a strong horse; there are no bounds to a wise man's knowledge."

The stylized head of a horse was obvious. A stick man with a headdress, holding a scroll, was the wise man. The symbol for "strong" was a series of interlocking lines. "Distance" was a small circle with two strings trailing up and away from it, representing something far from a known location. Clearly this was once a workable written language, but it is now used only in Naxi religious ceremonies. The Nature Conservancy has directed grant funds to encourage young Naxi to learn their people's early method of written communication, so it will not be lost.

Nguluko itself seems little changed from Rock's time. My driver feared for the undercarriage of our automobile on the craggy road into the village, so I entered as Rock himself must have done many times: on foot, through narrow, dusty streets, past stone houses and cud-chewing cows. A young woman pointed the way to Rock's former house. Inside the spartan quarters sat the skeleton of his narrow bed, a table, a few pots and pans. An adjoining hut serving as a small museum held a few other items left behind— a saw, some chisels, a rusty shotgun, and black-and-white photographs of the explorer and his entourage in the 1930s.

In language as politically incorrect today as his panda-skin hat, Rock was often critical of the Naxi, describing some of his helpers as lazy and careless and the village itself as "charmingly situated, if not overclean." His long tenure, however, bespoke an affection for the place, and when away from it, he longed to return. Although he last departed in 1949 after the Communist takeover and died in 1962, he is still held in respect by the Naxi, including a dwindling number of the elderly who actually knew him.

I found one of them—or rather he found me. In Baishi a tall, spry figure dressed in a long white tunic and wearing a black skullcap spied my Western features as I strolled through the village. He left his house to approach me on the street. "You American?" he asked. When I nodded, he announced enthusiastically, "I am Dr. Ho, well-known doctor of herbal medicine. Come, come, I show you."

He led me to a repository of letters and testimonials about his skills from around the world: a laudatory article from a newspaper in the United Kingdom, a letter from a man in Wisconsin who said Ho's herbs had made his cancer disappear, a request from a Californian for more of the beverage that he said made his father feel better. A doctor at the renowned Mayo Clinic in Rochester, Minnesota, inquired in a typewritten letter about the ingredients of a tea given by Dr. Ho to a cancer patient "who is much improved."

I followed my host into a small courtyard behind his house, where helpers were hanging wild plants to dry and dicing roots gathered from the mountains. He seemed to spring from specimen to specimen, a cricket of a man whose long, wispy white mustache trembled like antennae as he talked excitedly about herbal medicine and healing. His exuberance at 77 was enough to make me want to drink his teas, made from crushed tubers and dried herbs. He spoke fondly of the man who had inspired him more than half a century before.

Stair-stepped croplands prevent erosion on the slopes of northwest Yunnan Province.
Despite terracing, mudslides and avalanches have wiped out whole villages,
leading China's central government to ban cultivation on steeper slopes.

"I was Joseph Rock's student," he said with pride, explaining that the explorer had taken several Naxi boys in Nguluko under his intellectual wing. As we spoke, his memory of English improved. "I picked up my interest in natural medicines from him. People here remember him as a great man who helped them when they were sick.

"He was kind," he said, then added almost reluctantly, "but very excitable. The slightest thing could throw him into a rage."

Rock's patience was sorely tested on his many forays into little known territory. His articles in NATIONAL GEOGRAPHIC are sprinkled with references to "dirt, flies, opium smoke, noise, and general discomfort," to "dirty children" and drunken natives. But he also noted the friendliness extended by locals and praised the fortitude of his helpers under situations that were difficult and sometimes dangerous. When he and his entourage had to cross a raging river by sliding along a rope, Rock noted, "Some of my Nashi men had never been across a rope bridge, and although they did not utter a word of protest, I could see that they would have preferred to stay where they were."

Rock's accounts of unaffected people living amid scenic splendor may have inspired the idea of Shangri-la. Although he sometimes suffered miserable cold and rainy days on the trail, at other times he wrote things like, "The air was bracing, the sunshine glorious; birds were singing and all seemed glad for life." He wrote of deep valleys and forbidding gorges and, raising his eyes to the heights at one point, he observed, "Looking up to the snow-covered crest, it seemed incredible that one could descend such steep mountain walls."

HAPPY, SMILING PEOPLE, cut off from the rest of the world—did such descriptions in NATIONAL GEOGRAPHIC plant the germ of a novel about a hidden earthly paradise in the mind of James Hilton, who had never visited Yunnan?

The market value of Shangri-la has Chinese promoters clamoring to cash in on the name. Lijiang was first to announce that its rolling mountains and fertile valleys were what Hilton had in mind in his tale of stress-free monks and eternal youth. On the side of a commercial van in the city, I saw the logo "Shangri-la Tours" written in English. Miffed by Lijiang's presumption, the Nujiang prefecture along the Salween River appointed a committee of academicians to study the origins of the Shangri-la myth, to see if they might claim it instead. Their research, they say, revealed that a plane full of British had once crashed in the Tibetan highlands. The survivors were taken in by a monastery, circumstances eerily similar to Hilton's plot in *Lost Horizon.*

Scenic though Lijiang is, discovery of a modern Shangri-la would be more likely in extreme northwest Yunnan, not yet overrun by visitors. In the rugged canyons of the Salween, the Mekong, and the Yangtze, the Conservancy plans to concentrate its efforts of conservation. In addition to scenic delights, the slopes may hold a treasure trove of medical cures. In Kunming I visited a grandmotherly botanist named Li Heng, who spent a winter in the Gaoligong, mountains next to Burma. Between October 1990 and June 1991, she collected 7,075 plant specimens. In the summer of 1995, she returned with scientists from the United States, Great Britain, and Australia. That expedition collected 7,000 more.

"We found more genuses that were new to science than those that were known," Li said. "Nearly half the plants in the Gaoligong are endemic to China, and 434 plants are found only there." She added that although local people use many of them as medicines, medical science has tested "perhaps half" for possible use. Among those recognized as curatives is the bark of a tree called *Taxus yunnanensis,* which has properties effective in the treatment of cancer. Another, *Paris polyphylla,* has proven useful in stopping bleeding from an open wound.

Collection continues, with 13,000 specimens gathered in 1999, including 263 different species of orchids. Of the fish collected, 53 percent were endemic to the area. Why the special properties to life in these highlands?

"My theory is that when India drifted here, it brought with it many tropical plants, which were raised to high altitude in the collision with Asia," said Li Heng. "So the adjustments to a new climate may have given them special properties. This a very old area geologically, and now it is one of the most isolated places on Earth."

I FLEW TO THE CITY OF BAOSHAN AND HEADED NORTH by automobile on the old Burma Road, valuable as a supply route for Allied troops during World War II. The hand-placed cobblestones drummed under our tires as we wound along the contours of low mountains above the Salween River, past patchworks of rice paddies and vegetable gardens. Northward toward the Tibetan plateau, the gorge became narrower and steeper, and the Salween raged below us in a white froth. Cornfields clung to hillsides too steep to grow rice. Cultivating these slopes tends to cause mudslides and avalanches, and some have wiped out whole villages recently, so the central government has banned agriculture on slopes steeper than a 30 percent grade. The new economic plan is for villagers to plant trees—for forestry, fruit, and woodworking oil—and to make money from tourism. Clearly the tourists were not yet arriving in abundance, the trees needed to mature some, and the no-crop rule was not yet being enforced.

Far from Lijiang and its Naxi, we were heading for villages occupied by ethnic groups such as the Yi, the Lisu, and the Tibetans. In roadside villages where we paused, small children stared as though I'd come from outer space. Many tried out their grade school English, chirping "Hello!"

My small entourage, consisting of a Nature Conservancy guide, a Chinese interpreter, a driver, and two representatives of the prefecture governor's office, took meals in village restaurants: open streetside establishments with low wooden tables and foot-high stools. In the absence of menus, we voiced our preferences: some boiled greens, a chicken dish, eggs scrambled with tomatoes and peanut sauce, perhaps some yak meat with peppers (not too spicy, please, in deference to the foreign visitor), and the inevitable huge bowl of rice. The food was delicious. I never had a bad meal in Yunnan—nor did we ever finish a meal we were served. A table picked clean of food indicates to Chinese hosts that you left wanting more.

FEW BRIDGES SPAN THE UPPER SALWEEN and the water surges too violently for ferries. Now, as in Joseph Rock's time, villagers seeking commerce or social visits on the opposite bank slide along a rope suspended over the gorge. Steel cables have replaced twisted strands of bamboo, and passengers are now suspended under a pulley wheel instead of a U-shaped piece of oak greased with yak butter. For two-way traffic, two cables mark each crossing, each starting high on one side and ending up low on the other.

I allowed myself to be fastened into the device, with two straps passing under my hips, and I was pushed off the high side. The pulley wailed against the cable like a banshee. I glanced at the white water below and wondered if the Chinese had made allowances for a 190-pound Westerner riding their thin sling.

To my horror, the pulley ground to a stop about 30 feet from the low side, and I hung bobbing and swaying above the rapids. At the direction of a Lisu girl, who had preceded me, I swung around to grasp the cable and pulled myself arm over arm to solid ground. Then I climbed a steep path to the high platform above, settled the sling around my hips again, and slid across the river to the low spot on the opposite bank, making it all the way this time without pause.

Car travel, like rope-bridge crossing, is not for the fainthearted. The cliffside roads let two cars pass, but no guardrails allow for driver error. When traveling on the outside lane, passengers are best advised to avoid looking over the edge—the view shoots nearly straight down for perhaps 500 feet to the raging river. The road surface was often pitted or partially washed out, a mixed blessing, for while it made for rough riding, it also prevented our driver from gaining much speed. Locals assigned to maintain a stretch of highway were often at roadside with a wheelbarrow, shoveling gravel into depressions.

We paused often to let front-end loaders clear the rock from landslides that had spilled down the mountainsides. Evidence of recent ones averaged better than two per mile, for fall rains loosen the soil and create more landslides than in summer. Fall also calls for celebration of the year's crops. I was invited to a harvest festival at Baihualin, a Lisu village of some 850 perched on the steep slopes far above the Salween.

What a reception! They had built an arch of pine boughs over the path into the village. I walked through, then down a double line of welcoming singers, who directed me to a small church and a front pew. Men filed by with smiles, murmured greetings, shook hands. Wizened women grasped my hand in both of theirs and extended fervent welcomes in their tribal tongue. A choir dressed in bright Lisu costume gathered in front, a director raised his arms, and to my amazement they launched into the Hallelujah Chorus from Handel's *Messiah*—in Lisu! Also offered were a Lisu version of the hymn,

"Oh for a Thousand Tongues to Speak," a Thanksgiving hymn, and "Auld Lang Syne."

At the concert's conclusion, villagers crowded around with more smiles and what seemed like 850 handshakes. Their church, and their music, had been the work of Protestant missionaries from long ago, perhaps at the first of the 20th century, so long ago that their memories about the origins had dimmed. Chinese Communists had discouraged Christian beliefs, but this village parish thrived in its remoteness, shut off even from the Western missionaries who had founded it.

I descended the slope and returned to the road and more automobile travel, which one of my Chinese companions described as "discotheque" because of the gyrations it induces in passengers. But the views were riveting: high green ridges, plunging to the water's edge and spiced with numerous geologic oddities. At a roadside stand, young guides were selling tickets to enter caves that tunnel more than ten kilometers into a hillside.

Another stop offered views of Moon Rock, a perfectly round hole in a distant ridge through which one can see blue sky. As with most unusual geographic features, a legend surrounds its existence. The hole, it is told, was shot through by the arrow of a divine shepherd named Adeng to let out seawater after a dragon king had flooded the inland.

Tiger Leaping Rock is equally evocative. Water surging over the boulder in the middle of the Salween imitates the sinuous leap of a big cat, and thus was born the story of a tiger carrying a young man to union with his true love. The Flying Rock attraction within a small village is a true story no less preposterous than legend. In 1985, a boulder 20 feet thick tumbled down the slopes of the gorge, vaulted into the air, and landed smack in the middle of a family courtyard, sparing the surrounding living quarters.

The steeper the gorges, the more spectacular the scenery, but also the more frequent the washouts and the more likely the landslides. At one point, a huge slide had swept completely across the entire road, and a bumpy path had been re-created for a 200-yard stretch over the rubble. More loose rock appeared to be on its way.

It had been drizzling rain all morning, and when we reached the spot in early afternoon, loose stones big enough to dent a car or bash through a windshield were tumbling periodically across the improvised one-way track, signaling further loosening of the mountainside above. A half dozen vehicles were parked at either side of the landslide, their drivers worrying either about the rolling stones or about the entire roadway suddenly sliding into the river. As we paused to reconnoiter, two Lisu women in colorful costume came walking along the road, surveyed the slide area, and turned around to walk back the way they came. Not a good sign—but we elected to go for it.

I hung out the window, watching for tumbling stones to dodge, as our driver picked his way over the jumbled debris. For a tense 30 seconds we bounced along, until we reached decent road again and sped on. Not the most prudent decision, perhaps, but there was much country to cover and limited time in which to see it. Also, somewhere up ahead, a young Lisu girl was waiting to have a drink with me. Out of the same cup. At the same time.

INVITED TO A BANQUET IN A FAMILY COMPOUND in the town of Fugong, I encountered hospitality as fervent as that experienced at the Baihualin church, if less spiritual. I mounted a long flight of stone steps and was met at the entrance by two young girls in their late teens or early twenties, singing a greeting that included an invitation to drink. They handed me a wooden tumbler filled with a cloudy sorghum mash, which I was encouraged to toss back with one swallow.

They led our party to a raised rattan dining room with small stools set in a circle. Soon dishes of food appeared in the center, and we dug in with chopsticks. The girls reappeared, singing their songs of hospitality. This time they wanted to drink with me in a way much more intimate than merely raising two glasses together. One filled a tumbler with the liquid, put her cheek next to mine, and together we drained the cup.

The Lisu believe excess in the swilling of their fermented liquid is an honorable act. I left the compound loaded with honor—so loaded that a member of the family lent a steadying hand as I descended the stone stairs to the road below.

Landslides precluded any car travel beyond Gongshan, a town of 8,000. A pleasant walk down the main street one evening to numerous cheerful greetings ("Hello!") revealed that streetlights had not yet made their appearance, although preparations for tourists had. Over another lunch of mind-boggling variety, a local tourist board official told me that six million yuan ($750,000) is being spent to build visitor lodges, hotels, and signs pointing the way to local attractions. Wild dulong cattle live in the surrounding hills, and some would be confined in areas where tourists could see them, like our bison in American parks. Walking paths with day-long hikes would allow visitors to explore the ridges above the town. Logging had been the main source of income in years past, he said, but with a recent ban on tree-felling in the province (again, to prevent landslides), the economy was turning to tourism.

What would a former sawyer do to earn a living, I asked, with his livelihood made illegal? "He might be retrained to open a restaurant to serve local food to tourists," the official answered, "or make local crafts for them to buy."

He offered to take me to one focus area of great beauty, a green valley with colorful villages, Buddhist temples, and Christian churches, where accommodations are being built for the expected visitors. But after a scenic drive of some miles, the way was blocked by the remains of a landslide that covered the entire road, and we had to turn back. This Shangri-la would have to wait for the front-end loaders.

I ENTERED MY SHANGRI-LA ON A MULE'S BACK, but getting back to the mule required several more days in the car. As the raven flies, over high mountains, Gongshan and Yubeng lay little more than 50 miles apart. Swept-away roads, unfortunately, required a retreat of several days back down the Salween and up the gorges of the Yangtze and the Mekong to reach the quiet valley where wolves announced the dawn.

In the long detour our car passed over the Zhongdian Plateau, an arid, treeless highland where the people were mostly round-faced Tibetans, renowned for their horsemanship. For centuries their caravans were the only means of supply for people in the mountainous far north of Yunnan. A new highway has put them out of business, but high-country Tibetans are now the favored drivers for trucks that grind up steep inclines and negotiate hairpin turns.

Our driver was not among them. Unaccustomed to the fuel demands of ridge climbing, he ran out of gasoline on a high slope, hours from any service station, with a frigid night approaching. Just before dark, a local bus chugged to a stop besides us. We squeezed in with a crowd of chain-smoking passengers for a murky, hours-long ride to the town of Dequin, leaving behind our chastened driver with the promise of sending someone back with fuel.

Nestled at just over 10,000 feet in the crook of a mountain arm, Dequin sits poised for a tourist onslaught that seems inevitable—and probably necessary, due to the logging prohibition. On clear days, the mountainous views include snow-covered Meili, and tour groups now organize day trips to the snowfields and overnight treks into the hills beyond.

"The ban on logging has brought hardship to our workers," said the county governor, Wujindingzeng. "Our top objective now is to develop the tourism potential while preserving the biological and cultural integrity of the area."

To see what needed to be preserved, I joined half a dozen Americans on a donkey caravan to the village of Yubeng, over the mountains. Carol Fox, the Conservancy staff member who first worked with the Chinese to found the Yunnan Great Rivers Project, led the trip.

"A Bangkok developer had wanted to open a ski resort in Yunnan a few years ago," she told me, explaining the organization's involvement in the area. "He realized that conditions weren't right for the resort, became interested in creating a national park, and contacted The Nature Conservancy. Over the next two years, he hosted our visits to the area to meet with Chinese government officials, who were interested in our ideas. We subsequently signed a memo of understanding to create a joint project office to protect the area's biological and cultural diversity while nurturing compatible economic development."

With Carol and members of her family—a daughter and her husband, a son and his lady companion—I mounted and headed up seemingly endless switchbacks on hills above the Mekong. Our animals showed practical, asslike reluctance at carrying our well-fed bodies up the steep incline, and they paused every 12 to 14 steps. Their owners let them blow a few seconds before urging them on with a whispered word that sounded like "chew."

The path measured perhaps two yards wide, with its outside edge an ominous-looking drop-off, partly studded by brush and young trees. The legendary wisdom and surefootedness of the donkey world comforted me—until my animal twice let one foot slip over the edge . . . and caught himself with the other three. After nearly three hours of climbing, we found ourselves at the ridge top, ducking under prayer flags tied to the trees by Buddhist pilgrims. Supplications to their gods are best made after arduous toil to a high point. We met several of them walking on the trail and, rather than showing resentment at our easier mode of travel, they smiled and extended one hand, palm upward, moving it up and down several times in a gesture that means "Peace be with you."

A furry black snub-nosed monkey cradles her skeptical offspring as humans intrude in their Yunnan habitat. Logging has fragmented it into separate forest islands, reducing these monkeys' numbers to fewer than 2,000. Logging bans and other protections are gradually bringing them back.

THE JOURNEY DOWN THE MOUNTAIN proved as unnerving as the journey coming up. I leaned far back in the saddle to give my donkey rear-end traction but still felt his hooves skidding occasionally. Twice I dismounted and walked for 20 minutes to give his legs and my rear a break. Finally roofs of houses showed far below, and we rode into the village of Yubeng in late afternoon. An elderly grandmother, tending a babe strapped to her back with cloths, watched us pass by her hut, muttering something in Tibetan that sounded like, "My, my, my, my, my!"

As the story goes (and there seems to be one for every Chinese location), for years no one beyond the mountains knew from what village the strangers came who showed up occasionally to trade for supplies. When one purchased a sack of potatoes one day, merchants secretly cut a small hole in the sack and the lowlanders then followed the trail of spuds over the mountains to Yubeng.

We rode into a small paddock in front of our quarters, a two-story hut of rough-cut boards built for the occasional tourists who now arrive. Sitting on benches in front of the hut and enjoying the magnificent view was a young couple who had preceded us, John Tschirhart (pronounced Sure-heart) and his Chinese-American wife, Karen Wang. Both are Seattle medical doctors, taking a break from practice. After I had settled into my room, I joined them on the bench and listened to tales of their travels throughout Asia over several months. "This is what we were looking for, this kind of natural, unspoiled beauty," said John, gazing out over the valley and its sentinel, Meili.

What, I asked him, was the allure of such a place? Why do people from developed parts of the world leave their warm houses and hot showers to sit before an unheated hut with no toilets?

"Everything modern is something we construct," he answered, looking out on the mountain-rimmed valley where yaks grazed beside crystal streams. "You can't build this kind of natural beauty and simplicity."

That natural beauty could change if the magic words "economic benefit" hold sway. Carol Fox joined us to report that one Chinese official said his government hopes to send 600 tourists a day over the mountains into Yubeng, a village of some 125 people. What then would become of quiet meadows, clear streams, and brooding mountains? The echoed calls and guard whistles at Spruce Meadow in the Jade Dragon Snow Range came to mind. "We are suggesting that they somehow retain the high quality of this experience," Carol said.

So far, the low numbers of tourists seemed little disruptive. Villagers came one evening and danced for us around a campfire that reflected off their bright-colored native costumes. Others joined us to watch, and a good time was had by all, including the 87-year-old grandmother who had made clucking noises when we entered the village. Through a series of translators, from English to Chinese to Tibetan, I asked her if occasional visitors were affecting life in the village. Good Buddhist, she replied that they were welcome.

"I wonder if people here know what kind of change a flood of visitors could bring," said Karen Wang.

Do those born into scenic splendor and shut off from a faster-paced outside world bask in their surroundings? Or is that pleasure limited to those who have tasted modernity and found it wanting? In the mountains above the village, I found a yak herdsmen who knew exactly what he had.

We began a 2,000-foot climb one morning to a high waterfall hallowed by Buddhists, first passing by a prayer wheel built by the villagers. A small sluice directed stream waters to a paddle wheel, which in turn revolved a drumlike cylinder of yak hide. On the hide were written prayers that the world might live in peace. Around and around went the drum, keeping the prayers in constant motion, constantly alive, exposing them to all points of the compass.

As varying degrees of fatigue separated our group into separate clumps, the Seattle doctors and I hiked together. A couple of hours above the village, a young man waved us over to the simple hut where he was working the hide of a mountain sheep into a warm vest. His name was Li Zhong Dilu, keeper of a herd of yak that roamed the rich pastures of the mountainside in summer. He seemed eager for human companionship after long weeks with only a large black dog to help him guard his sharp-horned, hairy charges. While here, he missed his two families. In this valley where women are scarce, he and his younger brother are married to the same wife, while he and his older brother are both married to another woman.

"The younger brother farms the land in summer while I tend the cattle up here, and the older brother drives a truck beyond the mountains to make some money," he explained. "Such marriages would never work if we were not brothers," he added with a smile, "but it is an arrangement that allows us to live in our home."

He meant, of course, the beautiful surroundings. He enjoys his time in the mountain pastures, tending the yaks, he said, "especially in the fall, when the colors make it more pleasurable."

This truly was a Shangri-la, described by either fact or fiction.

As James Hilton wrote in *Lost Horizon,* "the valley was nothing less than an enclosed paradise of amazing fertility."

"We were as in another world!" wrote Joseph Rock during a trek similar to ours over forested mountains, describing scenes that we now encountered: "A mossy carpet covered the ground. . . . . All was in autumn tints, the maples golden yellow, others crimson."

And the air thin. Well above 11,000 feet, every step became an effort and every breath a blessing. At the very edge of the timberline, we topped a ridge to see a thin plume of water pouring over a cliff top some 300 feet above and breaking into fine rain before striking the gravelly rocks ahead of us.

We removed our hats and walked through the shower three times clockwise, as we had seen our Buddhist guides do before us. Icy droplets spattered on our heads and ran down our necks. Maybe it was the green slopes looming behind us with silver streams pouring down their sides, Meili gleaming in the late afternoon sun, and the overall numbing perfection of this unspoiled place—but I felt something close to purification pass through me. ■

palmyra atoll
portfolio

BLUE SCAR ON PARADISE, *a ship channel*
from World War II slices through coral
near forested islets. Otherwise, modern events have
passed by these isolated specks in the vast ocean,
leaving unspoiled models of Pacific islands
that we've always imagined.

SEABIRDS OWN the air over Palmyra, and sometimes a small piece of the land when an egg seems threatened. Isolated in the central Pacific, a thousand miles south of Hawai'i, the tiny atoll has escaped the abuse and overuse by humans suffered by most other islands of the world. A U.S. territory since 1898, the atoll served as a mid-ocean refueling stop for supply planes during World War II. Later it became an unspoiled retreat for a Honolulu family, the Fullard-Leos, who owned most of it and sold it to The Nature Conservancy in November 2000. Its less than 700 above-water acres remain a major breeding site and gathering place for tropicbirds, boobies, and magnificent frigatebirds, as well as shell-to-shell clusters of hermit crabs (right). Ocean currents that converge here nourish and replenish a rich life underwater as well (preceding pages), including at least 130 species of stony coral, three times the number found on all the Hawaiian Islands combined.

THE ABSENCE OF people left Palmyra with a treasury of mature plant and animal life. With no one to cut trees for tools, shelter, or fire, forests of balsalike Pisonia grow to a hundred feet tall and become a bustling nursery for seabirds every spring. Coconut crabs (left), much sought for their sweet flesh elsewhere, roam unmolested, the largest crustacean on the islands. The 50 above-water bumps of land perch on the peaks of long extinct volcanoes that once extruded from the ocean floor. Polynesian navigators probably encountered them but perhaps did not stay because of the islands' small sizes and extreme remoteness. The fish, coconuts, birds, crabs, and abundant freshwater could have sustained human life; annual rainfall averages 175 inches. The few metal and concrete remnants of wartime defenses slowly weather away, and The Nature Conservancy may restore some areas altered by the Navy to their original condition.

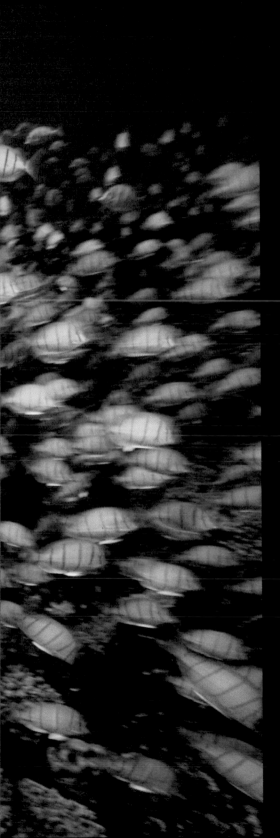

A BLIZZARD OF surgeonfish parts before the underwater photographer. Biologists marvel at the marine life that thrives in Palmyra's waters, undisturbed by commercial, sport, or subsistence fishing. Large schools of sharks, humphead wrasses, groupers, and bumphead parrot-fish, nearly wiped out elsewhere, swarm in abundance. Giant clams yawn unmo-lested on the seafloor and green sea tur-tles nest in beach sands free from human development. Palmyra could become a biodiversity storehouse of fish and coral, used to replenish other areas. In 2001 the waters of Palmyra were declared a National Wildlife Refuge.

A few ecotourists and researchers now visit, accommodated by a small, spartan, ecofriendly tent camp. Having bought the atoll for 30 million dollars, The Nature Conservancy plans to keep it natural, a slice of Pacific life frozen in time—like the weathered tree that floats in Palmyra's crystal-clear waters (following pages) .

The mission of The Nature Conservancy is to preserve the plants, animals,
and natural communities that represent the diversity of life on Earth
by protecting the lands and waters they need to survive.

The Nature Conservancy protects specific places where plant and animal species can survive for generations to come. We employ a scientific, systematic analysis to identify places large enough in scale and rich enough in plant and animal species to ensure meaningful conservation results. We call these areas the "Last Great Places."

At each place, we employ a range of strategies tailored to local circumstances. We buy land. We help other land owners manage their properties. We facilitate public-private partnerships. We engage the business community. We collaborate with like-minded partners. We seek pragmatic solutions.

By employing this scientific planning approach—called Conservation by Design— we are developing a blueprint for action throughout the Americas, Asia, and the Pacific Islands. The Nature Conservancy is committed to working with partners to protect all the places identified by that blueprint.

The result is a network of tangible success—places protected at an appropriate scale with the cooperation of local partners. Places that in turn influence how others pursue conservation in their communities.

Over the past 50 years, The Nature Conservancy has:

- Protected more than 12 million acres of habitat in the United States

- Joined with partners to safeguard another 80 million acres around the world

- Grown to be one of the nation's top ten charitable institutions, as measured by private funds raised

- Earned the support of millions of individuals and families

- Opened 400 offices in 29 countries

- Established a network of more than 1,500 volunteer trustees to guide local conservation efforts

- Pioneered land protection techniques such as debt-for-nature swaps and conservation easements

- Mobilized hundreds of millions of dollars in public funds to acquire and protect important natural areas

- Helped develop a hemispheric biological inventory to track some 50,000 species and ecological communities

For more information and to contact The Nature Conservancy
about the sites in this book:

The Nature Conservancy
Worldwide Office
4245 North Fairfax Drive
Suite 100
Arlington, VA 22203
(703) 841-4850

About Indonesia:

The Nature Conservancy Coastal and
  Marine Program–Indonesia
Jl. Pengembak No. 2
Sanur, Bali
Indonesia

About Belize:

Dan Campbell
Director, Central American Division
The Nature Conservancy
Worldwide Office
4245 North Fairfax Drive
Suite 100
Arlington, VA 22203

About Guatemala:

Andreas Lehnoff
Guatemala Program Director
TNC & Proarca / Apm
12 Avenida 14-41, Zona 10
Colonia Oakland
Guatemala City   01010
Guatemala

About the Poconos:

Ralph Cook
Senior Project Manager, Poconos
The Nature Conservancy
Northeastern Pennsylvania Office
Long Pond Road
P.O. Box 55
Long Pond, PA 18334

About the San Luis Valley:

Francis Fitzgerald
Project Manager, San Luis Valley
The Nature Conservancy
Medano-Zapata Ranch Project
5303 State Highway 150
Mosca, CO 81146

About the Yunnan Province, China:

Yunnan Province Representative Office
The Nature Conservancy
Xin Hua Office Tower, 20th floor
8 East Ren Min Road
Kunming, Yunnan 650051
People's Republic of China

About the Palmyra Atoll:

Chuck Cook
Project Director, Pacific Western Conservation Region
The Nature Conservancy
201 Mission Street
4th Floor
San Francisco, CA 94015

ABOUT THE AUTHOR

Iowa-born Noel Grove has been writing professionally for 40 years on a variety of subjects, but about half that time his emphasis has been on subjects relating to the environment. During a quarter century as staff writer for NATIONAL GEOGRAPHIC he authored 25 by-lined articles, one book and several book chapters, and served as the magazine's first environmental specialist. His journalistic travels have taken him to all 50 states and some 60 foreign countries. Since leaving the NATIONAL GEOGRAPHIC to freelance in 1994, Grove has authored six more books and three book chapters in addition to numerous magazine and newspaper articles. He lectures often, and has spoken before events such as a convention of the New York State United Teachers, the American Hospital Association's annual meeting, and the President George Bush Environmental Awards in Washington, D.C. He has also lectured on international tours for Grand Circle Travel of Boston.

Mr. Grove lives with his wife, Barbara, and 18-year-old daughter, Eleni, in a 200-year-old restored farmhouse near Middleburg, VA.

ACKNOWLEDGMENTS

Many thanks to Connie Gelb and Pat Rolston for their help and guidance with The Nature Conservancy's photo archive and in the search for photographers with collections featuring the Conservancy's work around the world.

Many thanks as well to Scott Anderson, Stephen Anderson, Fred Annand, Pauline Arroyo, Elizabeth Bland, Chuck Cook, Ralph Cook, Teresa Duran, Beth Duris, Karen Gleason, Suzanne Grill, Jennifer Grizzard, Lisa Henke, Pat Patterson, Elizabeth Reilly, Mark Robertson, Miya Rowe, Katherine Skinner, Mark Stern, Este Stifel, Rob Sutter, and Audrey Wolk.

Index

EARTH'S
last great places

Exploring The Nature Conservancy Worldwide

by Noel Grove

Published by the National Geographic Society

John M. Fahey, Jr.   *President and Chief Executive Officer*
Gilbert M. Grosvenor   *Chairman of the Board*
Nina D. Hoffman   *Executive Vice President*

Prepared by the Book Division

Kevin Mulroy   *Vice President and Editor-in-Chief*
Charles Kogod   *Illustrations Director*
Marianne R. Koszorus   *Design Director*

Staff for this Book

Barbara Brownell   *Executive Editor*
Karen M. Kostyal   *Project Editor*
Susan Tyler Hitchcock   *Text Editor*
Cinda Rose   *Art Director*
Melissa G. Ryan   *Illustrations Editor*
Carl Mehler   *Director of Maps*
Harris Andrews   *Researcher*
Matt Chwastyk,
The M Factory   *Map Production*
Sharon Kocsis Berry   *Illustrations Specialist*
Gary Colbert   *Production Director*
Richard S. Wain   *Production Project Manager*
Elizabeth Booz,
Cindy Min,
Jane Sunderland   *Contributing Editors*
Connie D. Binder   *Indexer*

Manufacturing and Quality Control

Christopher A. Liedel   *Chief Financial Officer*
Phillip L. Schlosser   *Managing Director*
John T. Dunn   *Technical Director*
Maryclare McGinty   *Manager*

ISBN 0-7922-2574-0 (reg.)
ISBN 0-7922-2579-1 (dlx.)

Library of Congress Cataloging-in-Publication Data

Grove, Noel.
  Earth's last great places : exploring the Nature Conservancy worldwide / Noel Grove.
    p. cm.
  1. Natural Areas. 2. nature Conservancy (U.S.) I. Title.

QH75.G72 2003
508--dc21   2002045173

One of the world's largest nonprofit scientific and educational organizations, the NATIONAL GEOGRAPHIC SOCIETY was founded in 1888 "for the increase and diffusion of geographic knowledge." Fulfilling this mission, the Society educates and inspires millions every day through its magazines, books, television programs, videos, maps and atlases, research grants, the National Geographic Bee, teacher workshops, and innovative classroom materials. The Society is supported through membership dues, charitable gifts, and income from the sale of its educational products. This support is vital to National Geographic's mission to increase global understanding and promote conservation of our planet through exploration, research, and education.

For more information, please call 1-800-NGS LINE (647-5463) or write to the following address:

National Geographic Society
1145 17th Street N.W.
Washington, D.C. 20036-4688
U.S.A.

Visit the Society's Web site at
www.nationalgeographic.com.

Composition for this book by the National Geographic Book Division.
Printed and bound by R. R. Donnelly & Sons, Willard, Ohio.
Color separations by Quad Imaging, Alexandria, Virginia.
Dust jacket printed by the Miken Co., Cheektowaga, New York.